Transcending Form: Ascend to the Stars

James Vissers

Wahpeton, North Dakota

This book is dedicated to Mother and Father Creator, Mother Inanna and Father Yeshua, the Divine, and all those in spirit who graced me with their presence and trusted me as a conduit for their messages. To my associates at Divine Healing Heart Ministry who believed in me and the unbelievable amount of love, support, and guidance through the twists and turns of my journey. To the wonderful artist who put words into motion and animated them with grace. To my mother and father who allowed, accepted, and appreciated me; inspired a love that spoke to the spark of my soul; picked me up and welcomed me home, my love is yours, forever and ever. To my family and friends, whose company brings me joy and fills my heart. To all of you, I am eternally grateful; this project would not have been possible without any of you.

I also dedicate this book to the spiritual journey. To the rollercoaster ride that feels like heartbreak but really is the endless return of coming home to our true self. May these divinely inspired messages guide all who are seeking Divine truth. May that Divine truth set you free. With that freedom, may you soar to the highest heights. Wherever your dreams may guide you, go in a good way, do no harm, and go with the kindness to hold the door open for all who seek that freedom. Do so in the name of the one true infinite creator, for one day we will walk side by side and have the opportunity to share the gifts and abilities of our soul's mission. May that day be full with the blessings of life everlasting.

— James

Dear heavenly Mother, Father Creator, Yeshua, and Inanna, associates of Divine Healing Heart Ministry, Guides, Guardians, Ancestors, Elders, and Soul Tribe: I just want to say thank you; thank you for all you have done and continue to do. Thank you for the guidance and support for the ups, downs, all of it, for the falling apart and falling into place, for being able to share a glimpse of the world through your eyes. Thank you for the opportunities you have brought before me that made me into the woman I am today. I have no idea where I would be without you and in all my existence I never wish to find out. Thank you for being you and helping me be me. I Love you unconditionally forever and always. See you in the stars.

— Rylee

Contents

Introduction

Greetings, welcome. Please, come sit and read. In these pages, you will find poems that reflect a journey inward and outward, a journey of ascension. The dates included indicate world and spiritual events as we travel together on a path to sovereignty. The poems are stepping stones. Symbols and light codes are included in the words. Along the way, you may notice new inner growth and begin to develop a deeper connection with your authentic self, and the world around you. The veils, which separate the physical realm from the spiritual realm, have been removed. A world without veils means complete transparency with the spiritual realm and the events that occur beyond the physical. Wherever you are on your journey, the poems will highlight the next steps.

Many of the poems symbolize a journey for Mother Inanna, also known as Mary Magdalene, who is here as Jaimee Barrington. The journey set forth in many of the poems was for her to walk and assist humanity in a collective ascension. In the section titled "Love Story," the poems describe the sacrifice she has made to stay behind and help humanity ascend. She sacrificed her ascension to stay on Earth and continue on the journey that her and Yeshua, also known as Jesus, started so many years ago. Much of the work has been done behind the veil, and much is unfolding in the physical world.

The journey is always forward towards the one true infinite creator. Know that we walk this path together. The path is a spiritual journey, and these poems can be used as reflective tools. Reading the pieces repetitively, and slowly, is to absorb the frequency coded in the messages. Poems that read like riddles contain layers of meaning. Reflections for further insight will be included in the back of the book. By reading the poems, and observing the painted art, you will be absorbing frequencies that will dismantle and cleanse your body of everything that no longer serves your highest good. The process may initiate inner work to change habits, behavioral patterns, and address old wounds and trauma, to assist in the healing and raising of your frequency.

The new codes will bring more light to your being, and you will begin to see big changes in your life. As you move forward on your spiritual journey, you may find aspects of your lifestyle that no longer hold your interest. Parts of you will fall away—say goodbye with Love, and move forward. Your diet will change, and you will find that you strive to keep yourself pure. This spiritual practice will help foster your connection with spirit.

As you connect with spirit, another layer of the journey will be revealed, and this will unfold as stages of inner growth. Look in each poem; can you identify the aspects of your life that are reflected in the words? What are the effects of the events on your daily life? Your day-to-day experiences matter a great deal, and as you pay attention to your emotions and behaviors, you will begin to feel like there is someone else behind these actions. That is the truth of this journey; the poems remove the veils from your perception, the mental and emotional conditioning of society, and the generational wounds, to uncover a more authentic version of you. With each step, another layer will be removed, and you will come to understand an authenticity that will become your new foundation.

As you establish your new foundation, you may notice the messages will reflect the world to you, yet they also show that the world is within you. As you search for meaning, perhaps you will see the clutter of parts that no longer have meaning needing to be released from your life. When you reach those release points, it's okay to release with tears. Speak a prayer and ask God for strength and to take away that which no longer serves you. Then be kind and gentle with yourself, take care of your body. Rest when needed and be sure to practice self-care and self-love. You will be discovering a version of yourself that does not fit with the current society. Free yourself, allow yourself to be caught in gifts and abilities and passions that you may have suppressed in your childhood, or just weren't supported in your society's education system.

Be patient with the process. You will begin to evolve in a way that you may not be aware of until some time has passed. The process itself is an eternal evolution involving constant change and growth. You may find guideposts in your natural environment.

Symbols will appear in the poems. You may find certain symbols that you connect with and utilize in your everyday life. Know that you can search the meaning of these symbols. Everything in the natural and spirit world is interconnected. For example, if it is a bird, or a flower that holds your attention from within a poem, it can be a sign for you to connect with this symbol in nature and see how it relates to your life. You may find that deeper meaning comes to you over time.

Over time, people will begin to fall away from you. You may begin to meet new people and form deep connections. Trust these connections, you are opening to people who understand your soul. You may be unfamiliar with your authentic self. Have fun learning about this person. Layers of who you thought you should be, or who you think you are, will disappear. Keep moving forward, this is the way with the awakening journey, it is ever evolving. You are constantly evolving.

As you explore your connection to source, follow your heart. Honor that connection. If you are feeling connected with rocks, crystals, or plants, then open your heart to that exploration. If it is drawing, then draw until your heart is content. As you awaken, you will begin to see and know a new reality. You are a multi-dimensional being who has family in the stars. Truth and reality will appear before you in various forms, depending on how you are able to perceive your surroundings.

Everyone and everything around you has an energetic signal, or frequency. Interacting with your surroundings will mean feeling other signals and emitting your signals. In truth, you are like radios, broadcasting your needs and desires into the universe. What arrives back to you may be in the form of thoughts, or outcomes, certain people, or even your relatives in the stars. This is a skill that will require mastery.

You will become aware of your telepathic communication abilities. They are potent. Thoughts and emotions can be sent and received by others, and you will have to be mindful of your intentions. This way of being will present to you a new set of responsibilities. Your thoughts will affect others, and you will sense that, especially when communicating face-to-face. Wherever your physical location, social or financial status, your inner life will matter most.

You will need time and space to spend in privacy, to tend to your inner world. See it as a garden within your heart that will grow to become your own world. Tend to that garden well. Be gentle, be kind, and be good. If you feel like you are moving too fast, take a break.

In that downtime, reflect on the truth that everything that exists above you also exists within you. When you go within, to that quiet place in your heart, you have the space free from the outside world. You can give yourself space from the busyness of society. The stillness will be your vehicle to travel with on this journey. This is your steed. You have only one steed, freewill, and one is all you need to travel this journey through the cosmos. That is another piece of the puzzle.

We are traveling back to the stars. For lifetimes, traumas and darkness have tied us to the physical planes of this planet. Over these lifetimes, our souls may have left to learn and grow elsewhere, but aspects and wounded pieces have remained on Earth. Many stories could be told about those lives and wounds. Know that those stories have been erased, and we now have a clean slate. This does not mean the process will not be painful—like any cleanse, the pain will get worse before it gets better. It will get better. See, even Earth herself is being cleansed, and on her surface, many are feeling her pain. What is Love without pain, but a library without books—the Earth, she only has one steed as well, and on her steed she sustains life. Learn from that pain, and treat one another well.

There is something to learn from every experience. In truth, learning and growing is how you can let the light into your life. Letting the light in will be important when you come into each new awakening phase. Whenever old parts fall away, filling those areas with love and light will assist in recovery and will strengthen your connection to source. If you are feeling down, or at a challenging point in your journey, learn a new skill. You are limitless in your ability to learn and grow and expand. Allow yourself to blossom on this journey. Boundaries, veils, wounds, limitations, separation, and lack, are falling away. You are becoming a sovereign being and stepping into your birthright as a multi-dimensional being of this universe. Your brothers and sisters in the stars will be your welcoming crew. You may trust in our faith and hope whenever you wish. Take in these words, and as you read, you will find more of these resting points to take a breath and recalibrate through these explanations.

When you see the word "channeled," it means that I am only a conduit, and the poem was inspired by specific members of the Divine working through me. Dates above each poem indicate the day the words came through the messenger. Those dates are benchmarks. For all who look back, the dates will correspond to worldwide events. Some poems tell of the events that happened in the spirit realm. The pieces fit together like a five-dimensional puzzle.

The dates are important to keep at the back of your mind. In truth, time is that 3-D illusion that stacks the veils in space and distorts our perceptions. The dates are celebrations to remember when parts of the veil came down. Windows were opened, and those who were awakened became more aware of the world, and the universe, the way our star brothers and sisters see it.

On a final note, know that you are never alone on this journey. These messages are channeled from our divine parents, guides, angels and guardians. They are always with you, and you are free to connect with them if you choose. You will have the chance to learn their frequencies through these messages. Once you learn their frequencies, you can practice the skill of discernment. They are also here, in spirit, to assist humanity in a collective ascension. In truth, it is prophesied that one day we will walk, as equals, with the one true infinite creator. We are returning to the void of creation, to live in a heart-centered universe as co-creators. That way of living involves unity, harmony, peace, Love, among many other characteristics. This is the future that awaits us.

Be well, and may Love be with you.

The Journey Begins

November 17th, 2020

A series of three channeled poems from Spirit

Poem #1

There is meaning
In speaking
And hope in the spaces
Between words,
Like the space
Between worlds
In the vast cosmos
Where meaning is
In the harmony
And the echo
Of chaos
As it hums.

(Poem #1, Blue Jay Truth, 11/17/20)

Poem #2

The blue jay turned
Its head away and the
Moonlight in its
Eyes cast a blue
Shadow.
The bird vanished
And left behind its shadow
In a feather,
"When you wear this on your chest,
Remember who I am,"
It said.

Poem #3

Shift the soul…
Ask and you shall receive,
To release from choice.
The power is unfolding
From the shackles,
To free generations.
The door is open,
Herald the chains,
Heavy trumpets sound.
The shift forward,
Victory pressed against the veil,
Creating new cosmos
In the womb of Love

November 18th, 2020

A channeled poem from Spirit

The ride takes many turns,
Turns that have dead ends.
Yet the straightaway is clear,
For forever has no end.
The end is the beginning,
You finish when you start.
Buckle up.

November 21st, 2020

A channeled poem from Spirit

Teach the faces
That face the teachers,
Grasp the sun,
Hand the light,
Squeeze the dark,
Pockets of mist,
Rites of wind
Flogged by tenderness.

November 23rd, 2020

1st channeled prayer from Golden Bear

Today we pray for the mask
Around our hearts to be removed,
No need to hide that which creates us.
To move forward is to be still,
To be strong is to be vulnerable,
To be courageous is to allow to let go,
To be full is to be truth,
To be open is to be one.
I pray that for today may
We be open

November 26th, 2020

2nd channeled prayer from Golden Bear

Today we pray for now;
We pray that the sadness be wiped away
By Mother's hands, her heart like a
Gentle whisper carrying our
Sorrows away in the wind.

We pray that the anger be removed
From our hands, the hot coals we hold
Against our hearts and wound us from
Receiving all that fills us up.

We pray that the despair, the stains
That tarnish our truth,
Be cleansed by Mother's tears.

We pray to be welcomed back into
The arms of our brothers
And sisters in the stars.

We pray for a helping hand to ease
Our feet from the hardships of
Our travels.

We pray to be cut loose from

Being there, past, present, and future,
So we can know the here, and
Hear the knowing of
Mother's embrace, reminding us
We are all her children.

And we pray that whatever
Heaviness weighs on our hearts
Receive the light of her being.

November 28th, 2020

A channeled poem from Spirit

Teach the three
Being alive is young.
Follow the gaze
Unwinding the days,
Trail the triumph,
Braided in the brush
Of the galaxies
Wilderness.
Task of days,
As the weeks are split,
Time is unzipped.

December 2nd, 2020

Two channeled poems from Spirit

Poem #1

Trace the sky,
And walk upon the stars,
The stepping stones
To the realm of the unthinkable.
Know this space
As the habitat for your soul.
Your home is there,
Where the lines
Between worlds expand
Into different dimensions—
Tunnels, for the soul
To meet the heart,
The core of creation.
Seek to know,
Breathe to understand.
Love to be,
Behind it all is you,
Tender of heart,
Tender of the garden

(Poem Series, Star Dancer, 12/2/20)

Poem #2

To meet at the beginning
Is to unfold at the seams,
And to greet nothingness
With open arms.
Climb the spine,
To the arches of the
Temple,
Where light has etched
On the walls
The story of your existence.
Meet me there,
And find out why
Eternity is as
Timeless as the stars

December 4th, 2020

A channeled poem from Spirit

The eye fills
The halls with light.
Forward, still.
Forward, still.
Lives are dancing on the walls,
Records of your pieces,
Keys to the lock.
In the mirror,
You are all of life.
To look not at what can be seen
But to know the unseen
Being, we are everywhere

December 7th, 2020

A channeled poem from Spirit

To ask the full question
Is to unlock the door.
Knock, knock,
The question is the answer.
Fill the cup up
And drink it down
Turn the key side to side,
Back to front,
Front and center.
Love all there is,
Love is all there is,
You are all there is

December 7th, 2020

A channeled poem from Spirit while at
Divine Healing Heart Ministry

Tail the crowd,
Fish the sea,
Bait the hook,
Crawl in the cave,
Twist the gut,
Stab the void,
Grab the helmet,
Bury the pearl,
Crack the horn,
Leave the tunnel,
Jump the chute.

December 8th, 2020

A channeled poem from Spirit

Take the magic.
Time is of the ocean,
Currents rolling and crashing,
Stormy seas swirling;
Pillars of echo.
The four corners are sealed.
Dive to the sky,
Swim to the bottom
And scoop the stars
Like sand.
Infinity in your hand,
Pearls are sprinkled
On the shores.
The diamonds shine
From the sun below.
You become the sky
And drink the night;
A new sun from your belly,
The core of the new earth
Dances and twirls in all dimensions.

December 10th, 2020

A channeled prayer from Golden Bear

Today we pray that the
Door once locked by uncertainty
Be opened by those who are
Willing to knock.
May the lock of doubt
Be turned by those curious
Enough to question.
May the hinges be
Loosened by those daring enough
To push through.
To be a child of God
Is to know that which is
In everything.

I pray to remember all that
I can become.
I pray to remember all that
I am.
Beyond that door
Is the source of creation.
I pray that I remember that
I am part of that creation.

December 11th, 2020

A channeled poem from Spirit

Lakes on fire,
Ponder the ice.
Spirals in the air,
Prisms of birds
Glow at dusk.
When the earth flips,
Doors in the ground
Swarm the flies.
Leave the entrance,
Tie the boughs,
Wipe the change
From the window
Of the sky.
Whisper your silence
To everything that lives.
Beyond the kingdom,
Blinders are on
Those who wake
From slumber.
The alarm is about to sound,
No snoozing!

December 16th, 2020

A channeled poem from Spirit

Time is in the wind,
The sheets are hanging on the line.
Take the string that echoes,
Fly to heights unseen.
Weave it in the tapestry,
Symbols of new destinies
For the waves forthcoming.
The stakes are high for all,
Time to take the laundry out,
To tidy up the attic,
Welcome in the guests,
Assist them with their tests.
Where we fall to pieces
Is where we come together
As one.
Many paths are crossing,
New webs are being spun,
The spider will time its fly.

Love Story

Love is the intention. Time has a beginning and an ending. Space exists for time to unfold. Love is the glue that holds it together. These next poems show the story that brings a tender tale of love that will usher the new stories to come. As time begins to come undone, creation will gain a new form. Creation will emanate from the heart. This series of poems is the story of Divine Father Yeshua, also known as Jesus, and Divine Mother Inanna, also known as Mary Magdalene, here as Jaimee Barrington. They have lived many lives together throughout creation. Tender are their hearts, for they allow, accept, and appreciate the tales and stories of old. They have endured much together, and yet their Love is endearing.

At this point in creation, choices have been made to come together in peace and unity. Everyone under the heavens has witnessed the Love between these two, and it has brought many together in agreeing to erase the old stories and come to peaceful terms. Love is the reason to forge new beginnings free from war, chaos, and power. Love has encapsulated these old dimensions in its warm embrace. They are being cleansed by the fire of these two.

The cosmos have seen her dance, and the echoes of Father Creator's smile have brought hope to the darkest corners. The tune is new, and sweet to the heart's ear. For what in creation is worth its time to stand shoulder to shoulder around their fire and gaze into the flames and see the gestation of the new world.

The sparks have flown since their first creation. Now, we stand at the horizon of a new era, and the eyes in our heart see through the sun as if we were one. In truth, Love has won, and what it means to create from the heart is to learn from these two, to read their tale from the mind within your heart. Read it slow, and sit by its fire. Let the wisdom warm your soul. To allow, accept, and appreciate these poems is to cleanse from your heart all that is the old creation—it is but tinder for the fire. That is the way of this transition into the new era.

Let the logs of your life catch fire from these stories, and see how space exists in your heart like a horizon that fits through the eye of your sun. Learn to live open-hearted, authentically and vulnerable to the heartaches of life. To live this way is to encourage growth and expansion of the heart. Receive this Love, and dance the sweet tune through the cosmos, where there is space for all to create life. Together we are becoming, and undone is unbecoming. The unknown is known by those with ears to hear, so hear the tale of those who have lived and breathed the breath of creation—the fire from their hearts. It is a dance for the ages.

December 20th, 2020

Series of eight channeled poems titled "And They Lived Happily Ever After"

From Divine Father Yeshua to Jaimee Barrington (Mother Inanna)

Poem #1

Mark these days,
Feel the trip.
Orientation in time,
Delivered by the North.
The South, delivered unto
The masses. Bring the town,
Forever the east,
West by the edges.
Tangled in chords,
Break the charm
Of the stars' wink;
Left to right,
Until the days break
And the moon,
And the sun,
Rise together

(Poems #1 & #2, City of Light, 12/20/20)

Poem #2

Task the night,
To the shape of dawn.
Fire on the boughs,
Bringer of ash
Begins at the opening.
Flesh to Earth,
Renewal of tissues
Dancing in the moonlight
On the beggar's crawl.
Fish to the bottom
Until the surface is full

Poem #3

Crash the ages,
Wind down from midnight;
Flashes and bangs,
Fireworks in the stars.
Date the moon
While the ticket is punched.
Freight of the world,
Details in the bills.
Forgive the cost,
All debts will be paid

(Poem #3, Water Sound Waves, 12/20/20)

Poem #4

By the seat of your pants,
Socks will fly off,
Uneven at the knees.
Matches unmatched,
Crack at the spark.
Flint to the rock,
Hard place meet stone
'Til the bells ring free.
Liberty and Justice
Tug on the rope
'Til the crack
Echoes around the world

Poem #5

Fates will meet feet,
Trail the dove's tail.
Flock to the sky,
Bars behind light
Shine on open scars.
Tick Tock...
When the toll
Comes due,
Paper will be fire.
Snow will fall from the streets,
Sidewalks paved in gold
Until rainbows shine true,
And colors hover
And tower,
Until dust is breath
And tender wind

(Poem #5, Lion Cub in the New World, 12/20/20)

Poem #6

Times edges etched in stone,
Tombs unearthed.
When the paw opens,
A roar from the desert.
Sand blankets the
Four corners
In the robe gilded
Green and gold.
From the pride
Steps forth a cub,
Flung to the wind
To meet the sun's kiss
And greet the sky.
Born on the high tide
Crashing coast to coast,
The royal fleet.

Poem #7

Tip the scales,
Weighted bills unbalanced
Touch Earth's core.
Flavors of sage
By the basket's handle,
Wicker and brass.
Tackle and bait,
Waders in the muck,
Streams clouded by night.
Blood drips from the pines,
Smoke billows from the
Chute of middle earth,
Guided by windy tunnels.
Flicker and echo
From the diamond's cavern,
Dishes to spoons,
Knives at the ready

(Poem #7, Rose Among the Flames, 12/20/20)

TRANSCENDING FORM: ASCEND TO THE STARS

Poem #8

Climb the final steps;
Rite of wonder
Washes the sky,
Dazzling stones
Awake in the fire
By the eternal stove.
Coal in the furnace,
Embers on high.
Frenzy of stardust,
Splashes of moonlight.
Haze in the meadows,
Twinkle in the dragon's
Eyes, fire tickles
The throat of the sky,
Alight in purple and
Pink sprinkles—
And They Lived Happily Ever After.

December 21ˢᵗ, 2020

On this day, Dibyanshu has visions in
my apartment, and two channeled poems
from Divine Father Creator and Divine
Father Yeshua accompany the visions

Poem #1

Flash the bones,
Warp speed through barriers.
Walls of vines apart,
Fallen on errant tasks.
Palms aligned at night
Fill the shoes.
Stars on treetops,
By the willows peak.
Draw the curtains,
Yule log on the stove.
Christmas tales,
Stories untold come true.
The fairest of the seasons
Is the bluest of the blues.

Poem #2

Falls for days,
Digging the trenches,
Bags of joy
Piled to the heavens.
Time will topple,
Trees will tremble,
Brambles will roll,
Phoenix on the perch
Ready to fire the gates.
To clear the destined door,
Months to pack
To fill newfound roles.
Bask in Moon's shadow,
Break in Sun's glowing edges.
Fly to the tilt,
To the final doorway,
Twist the bell
And push three times,
Welcome home.

December 21st, 2020

Two more channeled poems from
Mother Inanna (Jaimee) come after
Dibyanshu's vision at my apartment

Before the second poem, she writes,
"My turn to give the puzzle pieces"

Poem #1

You will fill these roles
The three of you;
Fly the destined path,
To fold the map's corners,
To roll loose ends.
Forget not the school
Will be closing,
No after school program
While the studies come
To rest
Of globes rolled.
Tuck in your back pocket
For safe keeping will come a time
When shadows return to light.

Poem #2

Cakes to bake
And lakes to make,
Celebration tidings.
Whisk away the gifts,
Love wrapped in bows.
Tiny shoes for new toes
Supple on the arches.
Black as earth,
Firm to touch,
Silver in her eyes,
Golden hair will glow.
Ride the tide
Until sun meets mountain
And the cloak of night
Is free

Christmas Poems

This written section was channeled from Divine Father Yeshua, also known as Jesus.

    The poems in this next section were channeled as gifts. They were meant to shine light on the beautiful hearts of their recipients. They are messages from guides, angels, and our divine parents. They are here to show how personal the journey can be, and how guidance can come in these layers. See, to each person these words carried inspiration for their souls. The timing was also significant. We were near a timeline that was ready to experience a mass awakening event. The planet has been back and forth a handful of times.

    The process is similar to a rocking chair. The collective gets to the edge of the chair and it is ready to tip forward and launch everyone into an awakening event. Then new events occur and the chair is rocking backwards and the collective is not quite ready for a big event. The collective was not ready at this time. This has allowed for more opportunities for healing and finishing lessons. The planet was undergoing massive changes and purging to lighten its grid.

    Total mass events are balancing acts, and around this time the balance was not there, but hope was being planted for future harvests. What a gift hope can be—whenever that blessing arrives, be sure to fill your pockets. Anytime these events are set to occur, make sure to store joy in your bellies. The transition of the event may be dark, and any lightheartedness will act as a beacon for more light to enter your life. In truth, these events could arrive in the blink of an eye. For the awakening masses, much of their trauma and wounds will erupt from their surfaces in an instant. Be mindful during these times. Give yourself time to perform tasks. The massive purging is not meant to be rushed. Be kind and gentle, especially to yourselves.

The mass event is meant to shake-up society and the entire system. Anyway, these poems were meant to inspire joy in the hearts of the recipients. Perhaps they can shed light on your journey inwards. Around this same time, a great event occurred; it was a birth of sorts. The birth of new hope, my precious sweetheart and I gave birth to a new star—a new world. The news is brought with open invitations to those who mean to join in creating through Love. This is a new way of being, and there was much anticipation for its birth. That is the new hope for the world—for all of creation. As you journey through this book of poems, hold that world and hope in your heart. Have faith, and be sure to say your gratitude, which locks in the prayers. We are well on our way to a new way of being. Be well on your walk, and give thanks for all that God has placed on your path.

Christmas Time

The poems that follow were channeled as Christmas
gifts, accompanied by channeled art from Rylee

The pieces were channeled from
the person's divine team

Some recipients will remain anonymous.

Comb the wheatgrass
Of your minds field,
Tie the chords
Of merriment
Through the drifts
Of snowy days.
Hark, the herald's king,
Moonlight across the snow
The dark winter fades
When the sun rises.

Lots of Love

****

Raise the rake
Of fall's break,
Tickle, prick,
Popple, crack.
Drops of ambrosia
On the eye's tongue,
Taste the sweetness
Of light's touch,
Palm the bough of life's
Cycle;
Support your nourishment.

Blessings & Glad Tidings,
Your smile is like the
Sunlight on a dark winter night,
You are the night's sun.
Lots of Love

Heir to the pen's delight,
Fair and thoughtful.
Parchment of the heart,
Mane of ink,
Voice of the light's roar,
Paws of stars.
Clasp the love
Of God's locket,
Treasured words
From the golden chest.

Our eternal Love
And gratitude for the ages,
Bell of the ball;
Your words ring forth
And bring hope on
Dark nights.
Love, forever and ever

Brenda S.

Blushing cheeks,
Flush on the rose
Petal, gold stems
Hanging from the heavens,
Taught on the temples
Of your beloved
Crown of hearts.
His love, eternal.
Rain or snow,
The endearing ray
Of sunshine on
The cloudiest of days;
You are my ending,
I will be your beginning.

Here always,
Wrapped around your
Heart,
Lots of Love

Leaves of change
Fall from the tree of life,
Flow through the cosmos,
Destinies gathered on the earth,
Crisp and fresh with
The heavenly scent.
Distinguished orbit
On the wind of
Providence.
Through the heart
The journey is channeled,
Love's tender hand
Carries you to eternity.

Love from the galactics,
Far out, and forever
Within. Love is in the air

****

Jaimee B.

Light of my rainbow,
Glowing through the dimensions,
Flashes of eternity swirling,
Pieces to puzzles,
Worlds apart.
Your key connects them
All, your light
Is the lamp for their feet,
Your love the path
They walk.
As the Moon's Sun,
And the Sun's Moon,
The stars dance and
Merge into eternity.
Words to Light to Ether,
The one of all
Mother of Love,
Dance with me.

Doves of Love
And locks of light,
My heart is yours,
Your man of bats,
You are all the love
That I am

****

James V.

Dive in the pond
With no bottom,
Loose leaves,
Shimmers unfolding,
Waters soothing
The fires that rage
And tear and wound.
Balm to heal and salve
To clear, what's open
Can close, what's torn
Can mend, what's dim
Can glow again, what's
Ash can rise again.

Our little spark
Of Love, We
Hold you in our hearts,
Sheltered in our love
You are safe to blossom,
You are safe to be.

Fly the jungle,
Tangle in the clouds.
You soar as high as you
Roar, take the leap,
Trust in your wings.
Your stripes carry you
In the wind.
Mountains and rivers
And oceans far,
One journey
Branches from your Love.

Lots of Love

****

Tara P.

Fleeting tasks take the cake
Baked with glitter.
The cherry on top
Will be the filling
Rising from the core.
Twinkle, twinkle
On a star, I wonder
Who the faeriest of all
Is.
Pink and stones
May shake your bones,
But your heart
Fills any cracks.
Shimmer, shimmer
In the dark,
The hope behind my eyes;
You fill me to the brim.
Icing on my lips,
You glow like the stars
Painted in the heavens.
Reach so high,
Flicker on the leaves.
Dance around the trunk of
My heart.

Dear Love, meet me at the
Forest's edge, where the sun and the moon
Set together. Love you through eternity.

****

Ron B.

Spotlight bright,
Nightfall falls away.
Afar in the sky,
The kite drifts
In the wind.
Lightning strikes,
Once in a lifetime,
Jewel.
Collection for the ages,
Crowns fall to the wayside.
Stride on, in joyful steps,
The ride, the slip and
Slide, gleeful on the waves,
Tickled by the light.
Rainbow hair,
Pot of gold
Starting from your heart.
Beat the drum
To the life you live
And give and live
With Love.

Dear one, You are the sparkle
In our sky, the trumpets to our ears.
Heaven's delight, lots of love,
Your family in the sky.

Brigette B.

Buckle up,
Light speed away.
Turn the page.
Mark the day
That dusk is met
With dawn.
Leaves are falling,
Twizzling in the sky.
Stars align,
A new sun
Born in your sky.
Melting you from the core,
Love abounds,
Milky in your sky.
From beginning to end,
Mysteries of the
Galaxy shine behind
Your eyes.
Spark at night,
Snap of iridescent.
From sight to blind,
Your heart sees through.
Breezy storm
Shaking the wind
In the eye of Love.
Be the rainbow,
Taste my heart,
Ambrosia to the touch.

Flower with the sword,
Warrior of my soul.

Dear Love,
Touch the sky.
Lean with the wind.
You're music to
The stars. Lots of love

Fields shining in the open sun,
Run for fun
Into the light,
Picking charms along
The way.
Fill your hands
With golden crescents,
And abundance will
Stretch your heart
Until your pockets
Overfill.
Take the leap
Into the roses,
Where the thorns
Of fortune
Are pure and true.
Where the sun opens,
The journey is endless.
Less and less
Of more and more;
If lessons are currency,
Then your exchange
Is Love.

Dear Son,
Whether the light flickers
Or dims, know that your
Brilliance within is

Like a star, and
Your uniqueness will
Always be a lamp for your
Path.
Bunches of Love, Dad.

Pitch the stars,
And swing for the home run.
A basket of beans
On a picnic in the sky,
Loaded with whispers
Of a fate re-sown.
Known to the hills
As mountaintops,
Overlooking the meadows
Where the dust rises and settles.
Find gems by the wayside
In the feverish hunt
For meaning,
Knowing is foggy.
When the wind of destiny
Shifts, the light will
Cut through
And your magical portal
Will be anew.
On the forests end,
A new journey begins,
Ripe with new love,
Waiting to be plucked.

Dear one,
To the renewing journey never goes
The spoils,
In the game of Life,

You are always
The trophy.
Lots of Love.

Pick the twins,
And pinch the light.
You are the dream
From which I will never awaken.
Bright and cheery cheeks,
And rosy bottoms,
Ice cream on Sunday;
Time plucked from the
Tree, free through
Eternity to enjoy your
Sweet heart.
Making most of the most
While the making is good.
Mixing the treat,
My heavenly delight.
Take flight on these words
And one day we
Will be
In the kitchen,
Mixing stars into our
Desserts.

Dear Love,
Our flight home
Will be a sweet
Journey, indeed. The
Joy of our reunion will
Be the cherries on

Top. Until then,
My love is always yours.

****

Rylee S.

Rite to flight,
Lies within the papers.
Comb the brushes,
Fluid in the colors.
Cleanse the pallet,
And flush from
Head to toe.
Graceful wit
And nimble toes,
Dancing with the
Wind. Ballerina,
Tip-toeing across the
Stars;
Change comes quick
With agile wit.
Brace yourself for
The leap,
For when you
Twirl,
And when you
Kick,
The heavens will
Alight with tricks.
To and fro,
Gamble not,
Fortunes made
From the heart.
Rich with grace,

When you expand,
Your dance will
Part the curtains
And the show
Will begin.

Dear one, your time
In the spotlight
Will be you shining
The spotlight on the
Crowd. Eyes will dazzle,
Tears will twinkle
And reflect the star
That you are.
Love, your heavenly dance team

Walking in Truth

Tests aren't meant to be passed or failed, but opportunities to learn. They may come in the form of dreams or situations in your waking life. The lessons can be open for interpretation. Bring any questions to your heart, and what you don't find answers to, pray for clarity. This is meant to sharpen your discernment. You can ask yourself, is this of pure love, pure light, and pure truth? If it is not, ask God for help in the removal of it. Is what is happening for your highest good, the highest good of the universe, and your maximum vital health? This skill can help navigate the challenges and changes in your daily life.

Understand that everyone will be undergoing changes. You might be questioning many aspects of your life. An important phase of growth will be to find and know your truths. Your truths will come as your authentic self comes to the surface. When that happens, strengthen your connection to source through your heart. Your heart will be the center when your head seems to be running in circles. These cycles are old ego programming, and it is time to let that crumble.

To walk in your truths is first to find them. The process of knowing your truths is a path that comes with practice. Let yourself be gentle in this unfolding, and trust that you can always go within. Make time to prioritize yourself, for the more you know that authentic self that you are rediscovering, the stronger you will feel what is true to you. Many levels of Love exist, and all will be accepted in the eyes of Love. To be true to yourself is to Love yourself. Practicing your truths will take time. Whenever doubt enters, remember that this is not truth. In the stillness, search for your truth. Then, in the noisy situations, you will begin to see beyond the chaos, into a depth of centeredness. Hold true and let this feeling be the guiding arrow from which you direct your actions.

Train your mind to question all that you feel, where it's coming from, whether it is your emotion. This will help strengthen your discernment. When you piece through the emotions, whatever is not yours is meant to be released. Working with breath can assist in letting go of those emotions. Wherever there is tension within your mind, or body, imagine that with each exhale that tension is loosening. You will begin to detach from emotions that are not yours. What will be left may be confusion, or a blank slate. Whatever the case, it is a good reminder to fill yourself with Love. Maybe that looks like practicing a skill or focusing on your passions.

You may notice a shift in your passions. You may be more motivated to leverage your passion towards a higher purpose, to a greater truth than where you were previously directing your effort. Notice how this may change your life. People might fall away, you may no longer be interested in your job, or the companies where you work.

However, this truth will be directed inward. How you begin to treat yourself when nobody else is watching will have an impact on your outer world. You may find value in more intrinsic qualities, like kindness, gentleness, and peace. You may yearn to receive these from others. The potency in this truth is that the more you treat yourself in this manner, the more you will have filled that depth within, and the more will be available for others.

As you learn to fill yourself, you will have a foundation from which you can continue to unfold. Sudden and new passions may arise, and know that you came with certain gifts to express and share. Your new truths may find an outlet of creative expression, or perhaps it is assisting in your community. If you are feeling the call to explore when you connect with your truth, allow, accept, and appreciate the inspiration. Utilize that discernment and follow your heart.

To speak on strengthening your connection to your truths, also practice discipline. Find a routine or strategy that works for you. If you need mental discipline, then set a schedule for yourself. Having this mental discipline will help your focus, and staying focused will allow you to flow in your truth.

To understand this flow, it may appear in the form of a skill set, a way of interpreting how you feel the frequencies and how you bring them into form. The flow may appear in the form of guiding principles. As the layers of old are shed and you become attuned to your authentic self, you may feel a strong urge that the system you are living in is no longer serving to protect your rights as a sovereign being. You may feel the need to protect those who are unable to protect themselves. You may want to help bring truth to the planet. Whatever it is, embrace your truth.

This will be the way of Love. We are transcending an old way of living into an abundant way of being. Know that when you walk your truth, it is the path of least resistance. Wherever you are guided to be, know that it is with a purpose. So find the truth within your presence, and be present with your truth.

December 23rd, 2020

A channeled prayer from Golden Bear

Today we pray for courage,
It is not easy to stand alone.
It is even harder to feel safe
Around many.
It is not easy to feel alone
When surrounded by many.

Today we pray to remember
That in the crowds of many,
We can be one.
We can be one being in the crowd;
We can be the crowd

Today we pray that the
Curtain of sadness be removed
From our hearts, the barrier
That keeps us disconnected.

We pray for connection.
Together we are as the
Divine Parents intended us to be.
Today we pray to look within
And see our family, dancing
Around our hearts.

Today we pray for the loneliness
To be taken away by Mother's embrace.

Today we pray to empty ourselves
Of doubt.
Today may we be cleansed of our
Fears.
Today we pray for solidarity in solitude.

December 23rd, 2020

A channeled poem from Divine Father Yeshua
and Divine Mother Inanna (Jaimee B.)

Fleece and fur
Mottled by the wind.
Pockets full of embers
By the world's stove.
Glide by the toe,
Feeling around in the
Dark night.
Glasses made of light,
Rays of rainbow armed
With pink darts unleashed,
Tethered with eggs abound.
Fleece the feathers
Until the bounty of Fall's harvest
Comes due.
Turn the corn,
Sickle on the wheat.
Stock the stores,
Reap what can't be sold.
Canned oil will spill,
And the wells will run dry.
Harvest the joy
And store it in your bellies;
The final winter is coming.

Our hearts alight in the sky
Like stars:
We are coming for you.

Your Guides and Angels

On your awakening journey, you will have at your side angels, guides, and guardians who are here to assist you. If you wish, you can connect with these beings through meditation. Ask your guides and angels questions and get to know them. At any time, any place, you can ask for help. Know that they are always there for you. Prayer is a tool that will aid you on this journey. Whenever you are questioning your choices, or needing someone to listen to you, pray and invite them into your lives. Speak and you will be heard. Whenever receiving answers, allow time for changes to occur. Time is different between you and your guides. It is your choice on whether to accept the guidance. Know that the quicker you accept the guidance and make the positive choices, the sooner you shall see the changes.

Your angels, guides, and guardians have names. Sit with them and learn about one another. There is a reason they were assigned to you. You can learn and connect with yourself on a deeper level by asking these questions. Some may be near you for protection, others for inspiration. Even if you are having a tough day, they will bring some light-hearted fun to keep you going. Any question is a good question.

You can also ask your ascended masters and teachers for help if you are seeking guidance with learning lessons. You have ancestors if you are seeking assistance for courage, strength, and support. Your divine parents will always be here to embrace you and bring unconditional Love into your life.

No matter what it is you are seeking, help is always a moment away. Know that even if we don't respond immediately, we still Love and support you. We may have to love from a distance while you are working through a lesson. If this is the case, you are learning development in ways that will support future growth. The more you grow, you may come to know an inner strength that is unshakeable. If you are met with difficult lessons, remember the blessings that will come, and focus on the light. Whatever you focus on will draw your attention. Be mindful of your focus. So, in connecting with your guides, you are directing attention to your heart. All that you need is within your heart, connect and this connection will be strengthened.

December 24th, 2020

A channeled poem from Divine Mother
Inanna

For me to meditate on my heart

Shift your sight,
Fool's gold is your lighthouse
No more.
Find the pieces that
Lie in your chest;
Mend and glue and stitch.
You have a heart of gold,
Feel its warmth,
It will be your furnace
On the cold, dark nights.
Remember, hope is that
Flame you hold
When the ships seek
The shores.
Lost souls will find
Footing
Where the path is slick
With morning dew.
Hollow in heart,
And feeble in courage;
Show them they can fly.
If they seek real treasure,

X marks the spot
On the maps pinned across
Their chest.
Find the dormant coals
And strike a new spark.

December 28th, 2020

A channeled poem from Divine Father Yeshua

Roots of the pine,
Scarred Tar
And torn bark,
Honey on the wounds.
Wind swaying,
Pain taken by the wind.
Cracks and moans
Swaying in the trunk.
Patterns and plates
Fill to the brim.
Felt socks
Stuffed with gifts.
Now is the time to unpack.
New buds to flower
In the spring,
When the meadows
Are fresh with morning dew.
Rising into fog,
Towards the sun,
Steam on the stove.
Kettle meet mug,
Pour out the night.
At dawn receive
The new life.

Superchargers ready;
Batteries are filling.

(Moon Star, Roots of the Pine, 12/28/20)

December 28ᵗʰ, 2020

A channeled poem from Divine Father
Creator and Divine Father Yeshua

Turmoil in the sky,
Hunted by wings.
Flying to meet
The fowl,
Marked by the high sun.
Reflections in the diamonds,
Glistening in the grass.
Shadows scream,
Towers fall from the
Horizon,
Where the moon is stuck.
Harvesting by night,
Cloaked by day,
Light twinkling at the core.
Switches flipped,
And doves flapping.
Kicking dust,
Rocks sliding from
On high.
When the valley opens,
Ghosts and bones resurface.

Taste the wind
And the canopy that
Warms the heart.

December 31st, 2020

A channeled Poem from Divine Father Yeshua

Town and country
Is the place to be,
Farm living
Is the way to see.
The old skin
Will fall away.
Meet the core,
Tender and mild,
Sweet to care for
And nurture
All the while.
Awaken the parts,
And sleep in wholeness.
Activate the lights
Hanging from your soul.
Miracles abound
When the juice is charged,
And the batteries are full.
Granted, and not for
Taking,
Giving times giving
Multiplies the kindness;
Ripples of magic
Sent forth with each deed.

Heed though
Which mouth that you feed.

January 1ˢᵗ, 2021

A series of six channeled poems

Poem #1

Channeled from Divine Father Yeshua

Little stars and little bells,
Little rings and little shoes,
Lines of bows and little smiles,
Pictures posted on the refrigerator.
Little boys and girls gathered round,
Listening fast, attention focused
On Mom and Dad.
Lessons taught and lessons learned,
Time to set them on their way.
New shoes for worn soles,
To carry them all the while.
Set with wings from Father's tears,
And Mother's smiles,
Brings blessings to all the miles.
Far and wide,
Sad and joyful;
We will be with you all the while.
We will be at your backs,
Holding the hand in your heart.

Shine your shoes,
And comb your hair,
Mind your P's and Q's.
Dance and sing,
Remember how to play.
Growing pains
And stretch marks
Erase with laughter.
Fill your bellies
And be on your way,
We're proud to see you go!

(Poem #1, Two Stars over the New World, 1/1/21)

TRANSCENDING FORM: ASCEND TO THE STARS

Poem #2

Channeled from Divine Father Yeshua
and Divine Father Creator

Link the boulders
That set the stage;
From slanted hills
To sandy windmills.
Freshly groomed stock,
Rationed from the heart.
Goggles on and handkerchief
Covers face,
Blind to fleece,
Blankets on their backs.
Footsteps straight;
Trust the wander,
Spirit will bring
You water.
Test the tomb,
Press the covers
From prophecies'
Face, unearth
The bones,
And resurrect
The treasure.
Gems of knowledge,
Buried in the scarabs.

Mounds will fold,
And paper will appear from rock.
Touch the stones,
And make a wish;
Forever is not
Long enough.
Grip the sides,
The sand will slide,
And fires will
Be put out.
Spirit will carry
You to the
Finish.
This is where
You will begin.

Poem #3

Channeled from Divine Father Yeshua

The stars will swirl,
The Milky Way laid
Before you.
Trust the North star,
Ride the tones,
See the magic
With your feet.
Let the herbs
Cleanse your
Body.
Lungs to breathe,
Filter the fluids.
Pack the grains,
Sandals too.
Flash and bang,
Watch the moon,
Timber.
Scorch the Earth,
On fallen knees,
Roar heard round
The world.
Clouds will part
On lightning flashes,
Thunder from the ground.

Crack the whip,
And send them home,
To the portal in the
Mount.
Sanai is where it is,
Where face meets eye,
And long told stories
Will be unheard.

Poem #4

Channeled from Divine Father Creator
and Divine Father Yeshua

Braided grass and glazed bowls,
Fried beans on tender heels.
Birds will squawk,
And hop the branch.
Monkeys will lead you
Astray.
Guided by the stones,
Ruins carved from the
Gods, long lost lives.
Freight in wooden carts,
Diamonds spilling,
Blood boiling,
Steam across the
Mountains.
Fleece and hats,
And woolen scarves.
Roots and medicine,
Chew it day by day.
The altitude will take your
Strength.
Pack the light,
And punch the signs,
Sacred sites behind

Closed doors.
Distractions heavy on the
Shoulders.
Boulders on the rope,
The team will link
And pull with might.
The fierce wind
Will smite.
Swords and chains,
Fire on the brow,
Anguish stirring.
Strike the gong,
Until the ring
Erupts the boulders.
Taste the sweat,
Recycled water,
Blisters on the palms.
Worn boots,
And weary eyes.
Full hearts
Will carry on.
Sticks and stones
May break your bones,
But your spirits will
Never falter.
Feel the warmth
Of each new sun,
And keep it close to mind.

What will be mined
Will restore all that
Is lost,
And the journey home
Through eternity
Will be worth the pain.

(Poem #4, Pain and Sorrow, 1/1/21)

Poem #5

Channeled from Divine Father Creator
and Divine Father Yeshua

Pull and push
Where frayed rope
Meets tangled leaves,
Borrowed time.
Steel and bones,
Flooded altar,
Crosses crashing down.
Holy tremble,
Shackles rattle,
Loosening the teeth.
Tightened jaws,
And muscle stripped
From bone.
Leaves twisted,
Wrap it around the wrist,
And fling the ring
From the task of duty.
Fire in the eyes,
Flaming shadows
And hollow footsteps.
Follow the chopped path,
Watch for sun's bite.

Walk the farms,
And pull the rations
For each day's new
Journey.
Flights abound,
Stretch your reach,
And pull the corners
To the center of the lake.
Sink or swim,
Anchored from the sky.
Dive deep and swim
To the door beneath the sea.
Salt will rise
On feeble arms,
Until the thirst
Is quenched.

Poem #6

Channeled from Divine Father Yeshua
and Divine Father Creator

The nature of strings
Will unravel from the
Divine tapestry.
Silk and fine fabrics,
Wet with solitude,
And tears of past virtues,
Wither to wisps
Of smoke from the
Hearth of the dining hall.
Family gathered in your
Warmth, good company
Fills the home;
A reunion for the ages.
Set the stages,
And share the stories.
Plays on words,
And laughter too.
Joy alight in the coals,
Smiles from ear to ear.
You are the air that
Carries the room,
And moves our hearts
To reunite.

Old grudges and quarrels
Melt away
When you take the stage.
Your play is true,
The story heard
By time.
What comes to mind
Is the heart's eyes
Coming unblind.
The feather tickles
Rigid tempers.
Watching your delight
In our camaraderie,
We kneel to you.
A pledge true,
To hold your love
Closest to our hearts.

(Poem #6, Divine Tapestry, 1/1/21)

January 3rd, 2021

Two Channeled Poems

Poem #1

Channeled from Divine Father
Yeshua to Jaimee (Divine Mother
Inanna)

Brick and mortar tabletops
Lend the mould
To copy and fold.
Card tables here,
Rocking chairs there,
A soul centered home.
Feast together,
Spark to the community,
Manners on high alert.
Dust the high places,
And check the plumbing.
Stack the cards right,
Tight as glue,
With all the new;
The foundation from which
You will build.
Cement the cracks
With Love.

A pinch of salt,
A dash of sugar
Until the cookies
Are baked through.
This home is yours,
To mend the tapestry anew.
Alight with joy,
And good company;
Faith and trust
Locked elbows.

Poem #2

Channeled from Divine Father Creator, Divine
Father Yeshua and Divine Mother Inanna

Guidance from my divine parents,
channeled for personal reflection

Cornerstone blocks,
And level ground.
Lay the stone,
Brick by brick,
Mindful of the soil.
Greet new members,
Clean sheets,
And fill bellies.
Tell the tales
Of budding love,
And the petals
Yet to unfold.
Light the flame,
And ignite the hearts
Of Heaven's expanding
Company.
Flock and herd,
Tend the spirits
As they wonder
Of a world

Free to love,
And grow the green
And tender garden.
When planted seeds
Become lengthy stalks,
The moon will harvest
Autumn's bounty
And clear the ground,
For next year's stock.

January 4th, 2021

A series of three channeled poems

Poem #1

From Divine Father Creator and
Divine Father Yeshua

Feathers of might
Press in the fields,
Tones of yellow and red.
Graves from the backyard,
Rocking chairs on the porch,
Little saplings growing in the gutters.
A place of peace,
Where puzzles fall to ashes.
Stir in the silver,
And press in the gold.
Light as a feather,
Your finger will touch;
All will become light.
The touch of a king,
To alchemists' delight,
To forge your bond
In a ring.
Marry me thrice,
And let the water boil.

Foil wrapped coil,
And steam from the cauldron.
Brewed in batches,
Ambrosia to the nose.
A miracle with each touch,
A butterfly from the cocoon.
Laden in silver,
And frothing with gold.
Pulled from the pocket,
Stored away in the heart.
From formless to form,
Bridging the gap.
From the limitless void, The
tale of faeries
Told true in your purity.

(For series of poems, French Cottage and Field, 1/4/21)

Poem #2

From Divine Father Yeshua

Flags torn,
Allegiances sworn.
Bravery is no match,
For the scales of justice
Are tipping.
Truths among truths,
False vows will shatter.
Lightning on the eaves,
And a dip in the roof.
Hallow's Eve in the portal,
To dine in the house,
White with new light.
Hope will stand,
And pledge on sacred ground.
New leaders amass,
And question the old ways.
Flights of new wings,
Pulling strings from the sky.
Promises kept whole,
No flipping of the coin.
All bets are off.
When the band-aid is pulled,
Old flesh will be exposed,
And scars will seal over

Freshly minted deals,
Signed with signatures
Of pure gold.
Truth be told,
The Heavenly order has arrived.

Poem #3

From Divine Father Creator and
Divine Father Yeshua

Scores and ranks,
And legions
At the ready.
Helmets flush
With heart shaped
Crests.
When you give the order,
The reign will begin.
Lakes of the tears
Will flood houses,
And streets.
A great ark,
Of a new covenant,
Will shine anew.
When night becomes light,
And days fall away,
A swarm of new boots
Will bring love,
Raining down.
Purple reign at the helm,
Pink flames of liberty
Aglow in her eyes.

Chest of gold,
With matching rope;
Our Commander-in-truth.

January 6th, 2021

Two channeled poems from Divine Father
Creator and Divine Father Yeshua
For Jaimee (Divine Mother Inanna)

Poem #1

Lights adorn
Your Majesty's crown.
The brush and snow
Clear paths can see.
Roots' edges
Lead you deeper,
Into the woods you go.
Deeper by night,
A fairytale moon
With wings.
The howls draw near,
Follow the pack.
Red Riding Hood,
With her angels,
Out front.
The way will glisten,
What's left is right,
And wrong no more.
Filter the sights,
Begin with the choice

To look from overhead.
Star bright, star light,
Orion will show you
The way.

(For both poems, Angelic Red Riding Hood, 1/6/21)

Poem #2

There is order
In the leaves
As they crunch
Beneath the snow.
Branches whistle
When the wind burrows.
The owl that watches
Is the one that says,
"Who is it, who talks
To this tree?"
Our willow friend burrows,
Snug in the mountains,
Where eyeballs watch,
Patient for movement.
When the sky reaches
Stillness, take cover
Under canopy,
And walk between the
Portal in the trees.

January 9th, 2021

A channeled poem from Divine Father
Creator and Divine Father Yeshua For
Jaimee (Divine Mother Inanna)

Trinkets of desire
Melt away in the sun.
Lakes of crystal
Show the way.
The moon hangs
In the reflection,
And talks to her.
Mother's two
Flat feet,
And willow branches,
Windswept skin,
And chapped heart.
Honey balm,
For the comb.
Tender spirals,
Sticks to tend
The fire.
Warm the toes,
And stretch the
Legs.
Some paths will
Be hollow.

Wind your way
Through each day,
And never start
Or falter.
Night will meet
Day, and hang in
Perfect balance.
Walk no further
When stars are
Smiling.
Here, you will hug
The sky.

January 14th, 2021

A channeled poem from Divine Father Yeshua
For Jaimee (Divine Mother Inanna) and
Brigette

Likes and hearts
Fuel the folly.
Sage the world,
To cleanse the waters
That move the hearts
From feeling to knowing,
And kneeling to standing.
To break the chains,
To be firm of back,
And proud to elect
A new company of
Warriors, bright hair
And cherry tipped wings.
Frankincense and Myrrh
Bathe their heads,
And kiss their cheeks.
To glide through choppy
Waters, beams cutting
Through the fog,
Guiding to shore lost
Ships, bringing in planes
To landing strips.
Fields gone dark,

And wilted bounty.
Stalks re-erected,
And full of marrow.
New backs to build,
New eyes to see.
Love meeting Light,
And hope greeting truth,
And faith smiling on the weary.
Touch the stones,
And watch them
Come to life,
And dance in the
Sun, across
The water, to
Revel in the moonlight.

(Angels on the Water, 1/14/21)

January 14th, 2021

A love sonnet from Divine Father
Yeshua to Jaimee (Divine Mother
Inanna) "Locks of Love"

Tender strength at the palms
Of my heart, still from
Lost days divided by the veil.
I sit beside you by the open fire,
Tucked beneath your woolen blanket.
Taking care to tend to the womb
Of your passions, meek as the
Tinder, longing to meet the coals.
The wind is dry,
Yet soft with your tears.
My heart aches as your
Cheeks crack, your hair
Becomes silver, and my
Heart melts to gold,
I locked elbows with you
And promised our love
Would never grow old.

(For Love Sonnet, Tears by the Fire, 1/14/21)

January 15ᵗʰ, 2021

A channeled poem from Divine Father Creator

Latitude and longitude,
Breathing in the atmosphere.
Falling upwards,
The gravity is shifting.
Beneath your feet will
Be the clouds,
Ever shifting in the wind
Of destiny.
Break loose from any
Solid ground.
While flights are grounded,
You will soar.
Flags for love,
And banners for light.
The eagles will take formation,
And tornadoes of
Change will
Send forth from your
Wings, flocks will rise
And will take to
The air in swarms.
Together, it will be together
As one, everyone drafting,
And banking and swooping

Behind mother bird.
Her eyes are focused,
Course set to new lands.

January 15th, 2021

A channeled poem from Divine Father Creator,
Divine Father Yeshua, and Divine Mother Inanna

Needs are risks
That will unfold
From the heart.
Where tales have told
Great stories of old.
But of new, the
Blossoming flowers are
Of new species,
And worlds,
And breath,
Rising from the heart
In new ways.
Full of excitement,
And bliss stretching
At the limbs.
Flowers facing new
Moons and new
Suns, a cosmos of
Roses, spiraling
From our heart,
Tickle the space
Between worlds,
Swirling from the

Chest of our
Divine Parents.
The tree of life
Will grow anew,
And from the seeds
Of Love,
A new forest.

(Tree of Heart Chakra, 1/15/21)

January 16th, 2021

A channeled poem from Divine Father Creator,
Divine Mother Creator, and Divine Father Yeshua
For Jaimee and Brigette

Tighten the braces,
And flex the branches.
Floating on the tourmaline
Is the topaz crescent.
Flecks of ruby
Languish the tips
Of the pines.
Wrenched from the center,
A jarring atmosphere
Comes down.
To wrap the presence
Of the stag
In a swathe of fur;
To test the balance,
To remedy the scale.
Scales of iridescent
Fish to feed
The famine.
Hooks with no bait,
The net of faith
Brings bounty
To trusting hearts

And bellies.
Comforting bells are
Chiming, to ring in
The new year,
Salvation on the tongue
Of the flesh reincarnate.
To build the newest ships,
To tend the newborn flocks.
Whips and chains no more,
Free to graze the horizon,
And make fill of eternal joy.

(Moon Buck, 1/16/21)

January 19th, 2021

A channeled poem from Divine Father
Creator, Divine Mother Creator, Divine
Father Yeshua, and Divine Mother Inanna

The herd is on the move,
Deer bounding here and there.
Pinecones rustling,
Dropping into fresh soil,
Prepare the bones
To meet soles.
Lavish renovations,
Interior meet exterior.
Spices of the seasons,
Sipping from the mug
Of Life everlasting.
Dash the halls
With myrrh and holly.
Flock to the gates
With gifts of giving,
And flood the town
With tools to give.
Unwrap your gifts,
And show the world.
Open your hearts and
Receive new bounty,
From a world worth

Creating, a world
Worth rejoicing,
A world worth
Caring for, a world
Worth salvation, a
World worth saving,
A world worthy
Of the Love of its
Creator.
A world worth hugging,
A world worth loving.
Be in good cheer,
The season of Now
Is here.

January 19th, 2021

A channeled poem from Divine Mother
Galaxy, Divine Father Creator, Divine Mother
Creator, and Divine Father Yeshua

Tides among the channels
Rip the currents
From the core of the universe.
Atoms + particles
Split the eye.
Feelings cost tread.
Alter the shapes
That shape reality.
The matrix is stretching,
New code placed for
Lost time, hidden
Between the fabric
Of now and then.
Fevers take the mantle,
A breeze washes over
The face.
Lights out, until a
New dawn, and the
Heart filters the new
Forms,
And what shape they will
Be.

Who these new beings are
Will alight the universe,
Interest the stars
From the corners of
Creation.
Take form into your
Heart,
And make anew what
Was once gold.
The new element:
L, for Love.

(Soul Surfing on Sacred Geometry, 1/19/21)

January 20th, 2021

Sagas of a new galaxy from the Angels and Heralds

Saga #1

The moon, she is talking to the stars,
And they are telling her stories that
Are sending ripples through space
And time. New timelines are being
Received into her being, and the
Trajectory of the planet is being
Altered.

She is showing them her scars and
Wounds from battles endured with
Her heart. Her shields are stronger
Than ever, reinforced from the
Brilliance of the Sun. They can see
In her shine a place awaiting the
Birth of a whole new constellation.

They are crying, and their tears are
Sending a cloud of dust forth, and
They are asking to be included in the
Creation.
"Yes," she says.

"Go forward and tell others what you
Have seen. This place is meant for
All, and all will have a place. For my
Heart is full enough to fit the
Universe."

(Saga #1, Divine Alignment, 1/20/21)

Saga #2

When the moon's shadow
Dances across the sky, she listens
To the rhythm of the universe.
Bodies in motion, and the darkness
Is still. Space never pauses, but
For the moon, inhales the hum
And flicker of light from the birth of
New stars. In their bellies, where
Galaxies are born, blend the
Tails of new comets and cupids.
The range is cast in glowing radiance,
Hot coals leak gas from the Milky Way,
Where the antlers are swaying, and with
Each hoof an echo of sparks
Stamp the seal in each new creation.
The sky is spinning, as true north
Adjusts, brimming with life, forms
Shoot from every angle in a parachute
Of dust. Music to the universe, as
It changes its sweet tune.
From the center, a new melody rings
Forth.

Saga #3

She walked along the stars like stepping stones,
Mindful with every step. She stopped along the way,
And whispered gently to each star –
That they will not be forgotten.
The galaxies spiral will spin a new way,
And the paths opening will allow for new pieces
To be added, and portals to leave the old behind.
Old wounds will sparkle with diamonds,
And the formations in the sky will shift
To foretell the new future. The new direction
Will send ripples of Mother's smile,
And her love will hold them on their greatest path,
Their greatest potential.
In the dance halls of the sky, they will clap
To the rhythm. The sound of celestial bodies
Will be the music for the dance. They will spin
Around her, and she will twirl beams
Of her Love brightening the halls all the while.
A new way will be born in that very dance,
A way of Love that will accept all of creation
As they are, no need to fight and struggle,
But to move and flow in harmony.
When they move, they will move as one.

January 24th, 2021

A channeled poem from Divine Father Creator,
Divine Mother Creator, and Divine Father Yeshua

Leeks and stones,
Bridles tied to the pony.
Taste the soup,
Pack it right,
So no stone
Is left unturned.
Pack to travel,
To the farthest
Reaches of your
Soul.
Tunnel in the gorge,
Funnels the rays
Of Love,
To activate the
Chute.
For the crew,
Landing is important.
Task each worker,
To limit your
Mighty journey.
Overwhelmed satchels,
Loaded down with

Filtered weights,
Of a transition
As slick as ice.
Slippery trails ahead.
Pack the skates,
Until next fall.
The gravel road
Will wander
About whom
Will wonder.
When to show,
And when to hide,
The hood of night
Has many guards.
Hasten your steps,
And dip behind
The cover,
Angel wings in
The rocks.
Safe you will be
To take the
Next turn.
Where lights
End, you
Will see
The tunnel.

January 24th, 2021

A channeled poem from Divine Mother
Galaxy, Divine Father Creator, Divine Father
Yeshua and Divine Mother Inanna

Decks and portals,
Beakers on open flames.
Test the coals,
Twice struck by
Lightning.
Eaves and easels,
The painter's drought,
Stiff petals,
Frozen from the launch.
Drains are clogged,
And plumbing too.
Tubes of Saturn,
Tricksters with tails.
Forked tongues
And painted bellies,
Brows of orange and red.
Taste the fruit,
Poisoned by the touch.
The stare of mortality,
The flare shot into the
Sky.
Roses falling,

Winter wilt;
New growth,
Blooming at the base.
Flags are flapping,
And ripple
Beneath the wings.
Carry the stones,
And shoot from the hip,
Divinely guided shots.
Broken bottles,
And muddy horse prints.
Follow the yellow brick road,
You're not in
North Dakota
Anymore.

January 29th, 2021

A channeled prayer from Golden Bear

Today we pray that the
Light be called in
To fill the cracks
From these turbulent
Times.

Where there were once
Burdens that created these
Fissures, let the stress
Be lifted from their
Shoulders.

We pray that for all
Those looking for
Redemption, may they
Find it in the grace
Of Mother's forgiveness.

We pray for all the
Wandering souls who feel
Troubled and lost in the
Muck, may they see
Mother's open arms and
Become unstuck by the

Hand of God.
We pray for mercy,
For all those
Who fight against all
The Love that they are
Deserving of, may they feel
Mother's tears soften
Their struggle, and open
Their hearts.

For we are all worthy
Of Love,
We are all significant.

January 29th, 2021

A channeled message from The Divine

When a kindness is sent forth from one person to another, a signal is being sent—a message from the heart. Big or small, the kindness creates a ripple. Someone who smiles, or says hello, or listens, or offers words of encouragement, or offers a hug, or support in any other way, a wave radiates outward. The trees can sense it, the grass, the plants, those witnessing it will feel it. Even subconsciously, if they don't acknowledge it consciously, they are processing the wave. The magic is there, letting people be free. They see and feel that they can also be free. That is the magic. You are free to access this Love, each and every one of you. Let these ripples fill you up, and you will see how easy it is for them to spill forth in every direction that you go. Go with grace, and ease, and see that is the new way, that is the foundation of the new world. It is already unfolding, and it is beautiful to watch. Keep the vision in your heart that soon we will walk right into each other's arms. Be well, and be Loved.

January 31st, 2021

Two channeled poems from Spirit

Poem #1

The pond of glass
Thick as my soul,
Morning clouded by
The muck.
Clear night shines through,
Where bottom meets top.
Waters rush to meet sky,
Where depth meets light,
And new heights
Catch sight of the stars.
The water lily
Hovers between,
And delivers our heart
To the unending waters
That sail through the night,
To meet the eye of the storm.
This is home,
The unconquerable test,
Waiting for the storm that never passes,
Passing the skies that always shine.
To turn the cheek,
And see each,

Side by side,
The diminishing divide,
Where strong arms wobble
And meet weathered legs
In the middle.

Poem #2

Shadows dance
Around the fire
In my soul.
The boy is singing,
Hidden beneath the
Blanket,
Where ashes fall
But never touch him.
The smoke is humid,
And the tears drench the flames
And feed the coals.
Burn the blanket,
And see the sky,
His body bare in the
Stars, flesh
Stretched in the constellations.
Born within,
A space destroyed
By its creation.
Smothered by air,
Pump the arms,
Kicking and screaming,
The door opens.
Take the hand
Of the unborn child,
And meet clear eyes

That see through my soul,
And see,
And look,
And watch.
The edges cut,
And the middle split
Right through the middle,
To the diamond core.
Born under the pressure
Of a new age,
Held by the womb
Of a new galaxy.
Tender toes,
And watchful eyes,
To see new life unfold
And sparkle even in the day.
To dream of night,
To tell the stories of
Time's passage.
In the books that have
No endings,
And bindings formed
From stardust.
Kisses of ether
Hug the void,
And the space between
Unfolds
To meet the end;

The middle, where
The story is only
Beginning.

February 1st, 2021

Two channeled poems from Spirit

Poem #1

Tightened aperture,
The whole that widens
Fits the mouth
More than the palm
Can grasp,
Feeds the mouth
Which isn't fit
For the heart.
Who the owl
Flocks to the
Tinder, perched
Over the twisting,
The sparks,
Until the ground
Is covered in shavings,
And the wind
Has wiped away
The pit.
These are the downs
That never come up,
And the twists
Bending between words

Like hope,
Hope for the mild
Rhythm of my chest
To come alive
Like a band of drums
Played by the drummers
With no hands,
And no tongue
For the appetite
Of the mind.

Poem #2

Locks that fall to the side,
Twist from the surge
Of thunder behind
Her ears. She hears
The crack, the tree
Split. One half hangs
In the sky, and the
Other falls into a patch
Of sunflowers. This is
Our sun, they look,
Covering the trunk
With their shade.
Her eyes close, and
The legs choke, and
Turn to stone.
She lays on the rock,
Her tears turn to
Rubble, and her
Skin is pale,
A shade of lavender
When the sun falls.
When the owl moves,
The stones shiver
From the heat
Of the shadows,
How brisk her

Eyelids open
And close
And flash like lightning.

February 2nd, 2021

A channeled song from Spirit

Here I am,
I am coming home,
Mother,
I am returning to the
Earth.

Here I am,
I pray for strength.
It is not easy
Taking tender steps
With a heavy heart.

Here I am,
I pray for strength
So I can stand tall
Like the trees,
My roots deep,
And tall,
So I can reach
The heavens.

Here I am,
Mother,
I am home,
I am home.

February 3rd, 2021

A channeled poem from Divine Father
Creator and Divine Father Yeshua

Little tufts
Of braided wheatgrass,
Shells and silicone fragments,
Dust and pan,
Sweep the closet,
Sift the sand,
The corners of
Every dwelling.
Pick the cobwebs
From the attic,
And sell the junk
For milk and cookies.
Clean shaven stockings,
Brats, belts, and bells,
Smoke billows from
The boulders.
Breath hot on
The whiskers,
Beware of the cat
Hiding in the
Trees.
Lay the stones
In order,

Left to right,
From top to bottom,
Follow the pattern
To the cave.
Pick up sticks,
The fire will
Guide your feet.
Decipher the symbols
Painted on the walls,
Of a city caked
In dust,
A city to be
Renamed.

February 3rd, 2021

A channeled song from Spirit

Here I am,
Walking home to
You, Mother.
It is not easy to
Step with
Tender feet
With a heavy heart.

I am coming to you,
Mother.
I want to
Release
My hurts,
I want to
Surrender my burdens.

I present you my
Heart,
Mother,
In your palms
I lay
My hurts

And return
Them to the
Soil.

With every step,
I cover my spirit
With your soil,
And my heart
Is cleansed.

I leave behind
These unwanted parts,
I lay down
Upon your surface,
And surrender my
Needs.

I sink into the earth,
And give you my body.
Take away my power
To harm myself,
It is not mine—
I give it to you.

I give you my spirit,
Tender and mild.

February 8th, 2021

A channeled poem from Spirit

On the heels of death,
Errant stars
Disappear in the
Smoke
Of old galaxies,
Folding in,
And passing
By
The eyes of the
Universe.
As above,
So below.

February 11th, 2021

A channeled poem from Spirit

Strange, the ticks
Of life,
Braided with
The wheatgrass
Of the heavenly
Fields,
Lush with new
Seeds, the
Breadth of the
Soil, to sustain
Whatever the heart
Decides to plant.
Tending to the
Core, the budding
Doorway to the
Kingdom,
Where you take
No more than
You can give,
And give until
Your soul is no
More,
And find
Within you,

The blueprint
To
Begin anew.
To stretch the
Imagination
Is no space
For the harvest
Of the heart.
To plant is
To believe,
And growing
Is to the mind
As death is to
Living.
The seed that holds both
Gives rise to
Abundance.
This is your harvest.

February 17th, 2021

Two channeled poems from Spirit

Poem #1

Pour myself over the
Honey
Of the bees
Who swarm
My heart,
And teach
Me to gather
Pollen from the
Flowers that
Open when I
Am present.
The presence of
My mind
Takes off in the
Wind like dandelion
Seeds. Take flight,
You errant thoughts,
And leave my stem
Bare.
There is less of me
To be disturbed by
The wind,

Yet my stem
Is green with
Envy.
For no more can I
Give, and no
More can I take,
But to sit out
In the sun,
And the shade
Of the moon
Is to want for
Nothing, but to
Be still,
Aware of my
Deepest roots.
Where they call
Home is the
Source of my
Dimensions.

Poem #2

The shadow that is
Cast from the greatest
Heights knows every
Inch of the soul.
To become the edges,
To trace the stars,
Is to unravel the boundaries
Of the great mystery.
Death takes you to
The healing floor.
In the temples
Are books of lessons
That play movies of
Lives lived.
The life between
Births calls forth
The great journey.
From desert floor
To mountain top,
You can walk
The planes
Of existence,
And leave your
Bones, bare, behind.
Your spark will live
On to the pulse

Of the everlasting
Drum.
Like it called me
Forth from a curled
Heap on the dry and
Cracked desert floor,
To pray for rain
To soften the soil,
So I could be held
By the footsteps
Of my journey,
Lived in reverse,
So I could find
My way home.

February 23ʳᵈ, 2021

A channeled poem about Divine
Father Yeshua, channeled from Spirit

Skin as gentle as
Horse fur,
His heart finds
The sores of my
Body, and his
Embrace is like
A soothing warmth.
The pond breaks open,
And the rays of the
Sun wrap me
In the cocoon
Of his arms.
His voice is
Hot, like a breath
From the furnace
In his chest.
His hair tickles
My shoulders like
Feathers twirling from
The sky.
His arms squeeze,
And freedom
Lifts me towards his

Smile.
From the wind, he
Smells of honey.
I feel the
Sweetness on
My tongue,
Like medicine
It soothes
The wounds
And aches.
And how I
Long to hear
His voice.
I'm still in his
Arms,
And his voice
Is everywhere,
Weaving every
Memory together.
Then I open
My eyes,
And he's
Gone.
And I'm alone.
The air is silent.
In a faint whisper,
I say, "don't leave me,"
And his voice

Is in the
Echo between
Words,
The hope
In
The silence.

(The World in his Arms, 2/23/21)

March 1st, 2021

A channeled poem from Spirit

Art is in the earth,
Where a whisper,
And the snap of
A twig
Sharpen the heel
That presses
Into the mud
A frozen
Sunset.
Time rewinds
The tape,
And makes
Master the hand
That chooses.
Take down the
Shades over
The rainbow moon,
And watch the smoke's
Serrated edge
Slice the sky.
Watch the stars
Crumble, to sit
Beneath the soil,
And mingle with

The crystals
Until we find
Them surfacing
In our feet.
We carry the
Weight in our
Knees, and
Lift hope
Onto our hips,
And settle the
Burdens in our
Backpack like
Books we have
Outgrown.
Until our day
Is dust,
And dusk
Unites with
Dawn,
For reason
To meet
In the middle
Is the heart
That brought
The two
Together.

March 17th, 2021

This date marks a big event.
A channeled message from Divine Father
Yeshua and Divine Father Creator

Tender little cubs,
Outfits of golden silk,
Ready to make up
For lost time.
Galleries of rose bushes,
Little rows of thrushes
Too. Catches and scores
Dancing the lot of
Merry webs,
And bright cherubs
Flocking to hear
The vows
Of the night's
Treaty to the
Daylight. Take no
Hairs and count
No blessings.
Halfway over the
Moon, to dine
On official errands

That are cloaked
By the veil
Of crowded
Halls. New buds on
The bushes, new
Roots to meet the
Core, two cores
Into one, lakes
Glisten with
The sun's delight,
Shimmering in the
Waves. When the
Wind stops, the destiny
Has changed.
Fleeting moments of
Freedom, glance
But don't blink.
When the end
Is flipped,
And the beginning
Is split in two,
May blessings
Bring joy and
Tender waves
That ripple across
The sky,

And match
Wings to feet
With heels
Hot on the coals.
She will walk
The halls that
Open the gates
Of time,
For a matrimony
For the ages,
Arms linked
To unlock
The stepping stones
To the eternal world,
Brought forth
From jubilant
Landscapes,
Beginning and
Beginning,
Blooming
And blooming,
Until the petals
Touch the heavens,
And the core
Merges with
The new world.

Let this be
Known.
Freedom rings in
These halls.
The bells will
Be heard across
Dimensions.

(Moon Garden, 3/17/21)

(Sun Garden, 3/17/21)

March 18th, 2021

A channeled poem from Spirit

Among the pines,
Where there is
No time,
Change is passing by,
And the stillness
Of the wind
Shifts the shadow
Of the sun,
And in the shade
The moonlight
Touches my toes.
I am frozen,
As the glass
Veil pulls and
Fades into
The still center,
Where my heart
Runs,
And
Runs.
Still in place,
To a place
Among the
Pines,

Where the
Pine cone
Falls
And stays to
Admire
The Changing
Seasons.
Where life
Begins
And
Ends,
To the place
Between,
To watch the
Earth move below
My feet,
And the sky
Shift overhead.

March 19th, 2021

Two channeled poems from Spirit, given as gifts

The recipients shall remain anonymous

Poem #1

Flashes and bangs,
Turtles with roses
Submerged in the afterlife.
Fleeting stars that
Dance across the
Rainbows in the
Heavens.
Tickled pickles
And red robins
Too.
Flesh by the
Pound and no
Matches to set
Ablaze.
Tinder made from
Bones, hollow
To the marrow,
Arrows catapulted
From the sun
Fly the flag

Of the crescent
Moon.
Tucked in your
Door for safekeeping.
When the eagle
Spreads its wings
The wind takes
The tail,
To dine on
The final meal
Is the mystery
Of its arrival.
Until that day,
May your appetite
Be filled by the
Direction of your spirit.

From your team
In the sky.
Hugs and kisses
For all of time.

Poem #2

Take place
The space
That fills the
Belly with good
Company. Antlers
Dance across the
Horizon, soaked
In honey from
The tree
That touches the
Sky, and talks
Of a language
That beats to
The rhythm of
The drum.
To the center
Of your heart
Ripples send forth
And deliver the
Manna for
The spirits
To be renewed,
And to live
To tell their
Tales, of a
New world,

Where the buffalo
Roam, and those
That walk upright
Walk on their
Hands and teeter
With hardened feet.
The blood that
Drips from the
Eyes soaks the
Ashes of all you
Left behind,
Emptied from the
Soul, to renew,
To cleanse,
To rejuvenate,
To live by each
Breath and to Carry
the burdens no More.

Lightest of Feathers
Brush away the pain.
Your family in the sky, Lots of Love!

March 22nd, 2021

A channeled poem from Spirit

Nights are calm
When the palms
Are fitted in
The puzzle
Of the mind.
Brittle cages
Made of roots
Gnaw to the
Bone, cut from the
Cord that connects
To the womb.
The arches
Of tears
Mark the
Entryway, fresh
With garland and
Hopes of new
Adventures wrapped
Around the crown.
Little princess of
The woods
Takes the hand
Of the sky,
And plants it

In the soil.
For new buds
Will bloom,
Of a garden
Made of stone
And smoke,
And the spark
Will catch fire
The sage and
Tendrils of remnants
Of lives lived
And sown into the
Earth. Beneath
The rock tells
A story of those
Who walked
With their heads
In the stars.
They saw the
Galaxies shift.
When the stars
Stretched above their
Reach, their
Ribs cracked and
Turned to rubble,
Of civilizations
Ground to molten
Lava to be spewed

From the volcanoes.
When the sky remembers
And counts the ashes,
The sun will blink
And turn the color
Of the moon.
The pale horses
Will tremble in hunger,
And ride until their
Hooves are plucked
By the wind
Like the wings
Of flies that
Drain from the
Eyes of
Earth's waterfall.
Where the fruit
Grow above the
Branches, life
Was hanging
To be plucked
From the cradle
Of Grandmother's
Elbow as she
Held it close
To her heart.
The first taste
Brought breath

As food no more.
The well turned
Red, for the clay
Was swept away
From the roots,
And the leaves
From the tree
Crossed into the heavens,
Where a map
Of the old world
Is cut into each
Stem, like a path
Back in time,
To remember
The origin of
Its creation.

(Seed Star, 3/22/21)

March 27th, 2021

A channeled poem from Spirit

Ether is there,
In the filaments
Of the globe,
And the whole
World inside the
Palm of the
Garden.
To watch and
Tend the new
Growth
Is to keep
Steady
The dying breath,
And to ask it
When its fog clouds
The sun and
Hides the stars
From the moon,
Why?
Why?
Can the hands
Stop panting
Long enough
For the feet

To taste
The dust kicked
Up behind it,
To know where
The tracks are,
Where the path
Has gone,
And with it,
Faith that a
Path is needed
At all.
To walk upside down,
With feet in the
Clouds, and eyes
On the ground
Is to watch
The wind
Shift directions in
The grass.
To live in the
Sky
Is to trust
The wings that
Carried you there.

March 31st, 2021

A channeled poem from Spirit

Turquoise wheels
On the Rainbow
Highway,
Death leaking
From the exhaust.
Leave the fumes
Behind to boil
In the heat
Rising from the road.
Confirmations in
The brush,
In the bramble
Bleached by the
Sun,
Of scorn frozen
In time
And stamped
Into the
Desert floor.
Turn to the
Wall of faces,
And mask
The hand
That points

The finger
And prepares
To climb
The sky.
He is flying
To the moon,
Where cold
Meets the warmth
Of touch,
And the glow
Of affection
To grasp
His heart.
Will his compass
Be true,
Will the star
Shift in the
Sky and
Re-align
All the pieces
Below, like
A crab in
The sand,
Walking sideways
Toward the moonlight.

April 3rd, 2021

A channeled message from Divine Father
Creator, Divine Mother Creator, Divine
Father Yeshua, and Divine Mother Inanna

Tidings of good will,
And gleeful tails of
Rabbit feet.
The hares are turning
White, and the thumping
Of eaves comes
On the night
Of the dry tears,
On the wooden
Pinnacle that bears
The truth in
Tender wounds,
Solemn to the touch.
Filled with grace
From Mother's tears
And swollen from
Ear to ear.
When the nails
Came down,
And brought
A hush among
The sky,

The delicate cloth
Was sullen in
Blood, drops on
The seeds
Made fertile
For a kingdom
Born in everlasting
Renewal.
The soil in the
Sky rains fruit,
Abundance on the
Heavenly slides,
For all to
Find on Easter
Morning.
Seek the hidden
Eggs, and watch
What unfolds
From the source
Born within.
For which came
First, the chicken,
Or the egg.
May the mystery
Unravel from the
Spark that created
Both,
And find

The limitless
Love that
Tends to all
Of creation.
Flocks of doves
And sheep alike,
I tend to all
Who gather,
And together
We flock
As one,
Our feet
And our
Wings
In unity.
No one shall
Be forgotten,
No missteps
Counted, and
If any knees
Shall bend or
Falter, we gather
Our palms and wrap
You in our arms,
For we are
Meant to
Travel as one.

April 6th, 2021

A channeled poem from Spirit

Tears pass before
The Moon,
Like vapor
In the mirror
Of the earth.
Fortunes of leaves
Turn brown,
And drift
Into the
Atmosphere,
Where they hurl,
And swirl the
Magnet of the
Beyond. They
Crunch and
Crinkle and are
Squeezed of
Moisture as they
Wait to break through.
When they leave,
They find their own
Orbit somewhere
Between the Sun
And the Moon.

Quick to feel
The heat,
Then the gentle
Cool of the
Moon, until
They find space
Enough and fall
To gravity,
Until they cling
Together like
Puzzle pieces,
And paint the
Cosmos with new
Additions that sparkle
With rainbow sparks.
There we go,
Reborn in the
Eternal mist,
To drift in
The fabric of
Love.

April 14th, 2021

A channeled poem from Spirit

Time is cut
From the cloth
That registers
The indents of
Lines chopped on
The surface,
To measure
The growth by
Hacking at the
Rings of new
Growth and
Taking a sample,
To test for
New direction
Like a needle
On the compass
Of compassion.
True north
Spins round in
A circle,
And finds the
Wind blows
The seeds
In many directions,

And fertile soil
Is the fabric
Of space
Where the
Turtle carries
Stardust in its
Shell and waits
To step until
They orbit
Just before
Its mouth.
Who sends
The next stone
But the sun's
Ray reflected
From the pond
Of the Moon,
Calm, and bright,
Even at its
Deepest point.
To skate across the
Ice, and trust
The thickness
Of her patience,
For when the
Sun is warmest,
The rainbow
Melts into the

Water, and is
Carried to the
Edges of time,
To spill upwards,
And collect
At the center
Of creation.

April 14th, 2021

A channeled poem from Spirit

Imprinted on the
Tree of Life
Is land unraveled
In the leaves
That twirl on
End and
Suspend in the
Summer air.
Winter comes, and
The leaves fall
Sideways,
Never touching
The ground,
But gliding in
A sphere, where
Life and death
Merge like two
Tails that petrify,
And sow new roots
That climb into
The sky,
And hover in
The distance between
Dimensions,

And the branches
Intertwine
To create
The new forest.
In the dark woods,
They camp,
Huddled around the
Sticks,
Ablaze with old
Maps
Cut from the
Cloth of the
Tomb,
Soaked in the
Tears of warmth
That echo just
Below the canopy
Of the forest.
As they whisper,
Their teeth are
Light,
And fill the
Sky with color.
Their shadows clatter
In the undergrowth,
And claw to
Part the branches.
They suffocate in

The atmosphere,
Where the gravity
Of the Sun and
The Moon
So close together,
The shadows
Are turned inside
Out.
The forest floor
Is brown,
Until the
Green Man
Returns.

(Return of the Green Man, 4/14/21)

April 15th, 2021

A channeled poem from Spirit

The city has me
Now,
The road will
Take me
Where all roads
Take those
With hands
For wheels.
It will hover,
And erupt in
Raindrops of
Violet fire,
And pink clouds
Will wrap around
My exhaust,
And turn the
Hurt
To ripples of
Meaning
On the walkway
In the sky,
Where the path
To the Moon
Is paved with

The dark roots,
Surrendered
To be melted
In the Sun,
And part of me
Will leave and
Never return,
And the chaos
Will find meaning
In the hope
Between worlds
Like the hope
Between words,
And in the silence,
The cries of hope,
And rainbows
Grow from the
Tears.

(Blue Jay Lightning, 4/15/21)

TRANSCENDING FORM: ASCEND TO THE STARS

April 22nd, 2021

A channeled poem from Spirit

Shadows of the
Mind
Hide in the
Forest like
Paper tigers.
The prey of
Time,
To run and
Find the tallest
Tree,
And climb
And climb,
Until you reach
The canopy
Of time.
Hoisted on the
Tallest branch,
To find that
You only
Climbed sideways,
And up and
Down have
Lost meaning.
The sun is dark,

And the shadows
Walk on the
Sky, green
With envy.
They swoop
Down to meet
The owl,
"Who
Is there,"
It asks
And turns
Its head
To look at
The stars.
You've misplaced
Your feathers,
And your wings
Are paper
Glued to
Your body.
You soar everywhere
In the realm
Of shadows, looking
For the light,
And there is
No sun
To melt
Your wings

So that you
Can fall
To the forest
Floor, and
See the
Fire dances
At every corner
Within your
Own home.
No need
To hide
From the
Flame you
Have kept
So sacred.
The coals burn
White, and
Shimmer
With smiles
From distant
Galaxies.
There is your home,
In the stars,
Within you.

April 29th, 2021

A channeled poem from Spirit

The place of
Will sits high
Upon the stone
Throne,
Where no one
With wings
Can leave.
Torrent of
Violet fire
Stream from
The eyes
Of the
Forgotten one.
When the memory
Returns,
The waters
Will spill
Forth
From the hills
Molded in
Her form,
The seed
That holds
The cup,

The egg
That carries
The ether,
It swirls
Inside the cup
And swishes away
The skin of the
Earth's snake,
Forever swallowing
Itself no more.
The cycle then
Reverses,
And from form
Returns the
Formless.

(Holy Mother Transformation, 4/29/21)

April 29th, 2021

A channeled message from Spirit, For Brigette

Wild feathers of
The bush,
Plucked from the
Wing of the moon,
Silently radiant.
In streaks of
Gold and red.
The owl
Rounds the
Sun, and
Strips the eye
Of its canvas.
Talons for brushes,
She sweeps the
Fabric
With the
Essence
Of her
Who,
And
Perches
On the edge
Of
Dimensions.

May 4th, 2021

A channeled message from Spirit

To stay open minded to bring about something that is for your highest good…it may not necessarily be the thing you thought you were looking for, or the way you thought it would be coming to you. Everything surrendered to the wind moves at its own pace. When the way is full with trees and branches, what resources the wind has brought you to. Maybe the way the light shines through the canopy is the guidance you need. You see it come and go, but it helps to lift your eyes from the ground. It opens your vision, perhaps the wind shows you how the light and the shadows dance together. Stay still for a moment, and here with your ear, the whisper beneath the noise.

May 10ᵗʰ, 2021

Two channeled poems

Poem #1

A channeled poem from Divine Father
Yeshua, for Jaimee (Divine Mother Inanna)

Jubilent triangles
At the hallmark square,
Hollow to the tips,
Where juice pours
From the eye
Of the tiger,
Flush the gates
With the language
Of the pillars.
The fortunes of
Man will splinter
When dropped,
Like the magic
of old,
When they chanted
In the woods,
and their spirits
drummed until
The moon

Turned orange
And warmed
Even the backside
Of their skin.
Truth is in
The vibrations.
When you fill
The space
With your Love,
The critters
Will have nothing
To feed on.
Like bears that
Step across
The water,
They lunch on
The bark that
Has fallen from
The sky.
When their paws
Touch the sky,
Leap from the
Boat, and swim
Until the boat
Is out of sight.

Poem #2

A channeled poem from Divine Mother Creator,
Divine Father Creator, and Divine Father Yeshua

Levees and dams,
Built to hold
And meant to last,
Filled with the
Test time places
On the world of man.
Lakes created by
Time are those
Everlasting shifts
That mould the
Surface of the
Earth.
Craters of the moon
Filled with life,
All the elements
Of creation.
Test the waters,
And filter
For the waves
Of charted territory.
Cut into the scene
Is the unkempt
Forest where minerals

Drop from the leaves,
And dew from the
Rocks meet in
The hearts of
Those daring
To unwind from
The cloth spun
Around your being.
Take the steps,
And let them
Wash away,
Look only to
The stars
With the hope
You will need
No more
For creating
On the
Imprintable surface.

May 15th, 2021

Two channeled poems for Jaimee (Divine Mother Inanna)

Poem #1

A channeled poem from Divine Father Creator,
Divine Mother Creator, and Divine Father Yeshua

Let the tests
Fall away into
Ashes, the coals
Of the stones
Will glow, and
In the silhouette,
The new path
Will be lit.
For days, the
Fog will settle,
And your eyes
Will strain to
See, but the hills
Will whisper
A tune for you
To taste.
In the wind,
The colors will
Spiral and catch

The leaves as
They hang on
The midnight
Light, and the
Shadows of buffalo
Will dance on
The sky like
Lightning brewing
In the belly
Of Earth.
Check your toes
To see the
Stars reflected
On your nails,
And in the
Gaps, the smoke
Will tickle a
New sensation,
Your heels will
Catch fire,
For you will
Dance the storm
That shakes
The sky
And loosens
The tar from
The shingles
Of every home.

(Poem #1, Thunder Beings, 5/15/21)

Poem #2

A channeled poem from Divine Mother
Galaxy, Divine Father Time, Divine Mother
Creator, and Divine Father Yeshua

Brushes and easels
Of every animal
Across the globe,
With painted tails;
A new portrait
Has been commissioned.
The colors fold
And bend, they
Crumple like tissue
Paper. When released
Into the gravity of
The new world,
The light is
Quantified, and
Registers a new
Hue. Blankets of
Time, decorated
With musical notes,
Adorn your shoulders
For all of space
To honor, that which
Matters is formed

From precious matter.
The infinite is now
The lightest, and floats
Through the galaxy
Like an Hourglass,
Waiting for the
Exact points to
Intersect and meld
To the pot the
Spoon from which
Creation was first
Stirred.
Mix the new palette
And prepare the waters,
Your brushes will
Be busy like bees
Swarming around
Your ears,
You will hear
The waves
And patterns
Indent the gel
Matrix with
A song that
Is layered in dimensions,
Encoded with the
Vibrations and frequencies
That will shape

A new groove;
The trajectory of
The new cosmos
That will shape
How eternity
Forever unfolds.

(For Poem #2, Animals through the Portal, 5/15/21)

May 26th, 2021

Two channeled poems

Poem #1

A channeled poem from Divine
Father Yeshua for Jaimee (Divine
Mother Inanna)

The lute strums
And chords of
Blossoms shine in
Pinks and blues.
The fountain hears
The tune, and the
Shadows of eternity
Rise from beneath
The rug. They lift
Into the sky and
Cast an iridescent
Silhouette where
The curvature of
The universe fits
Into the collapsible
Tunnel. The roots
Disintegrate and

Crumble to asteroids
And comets like
Little messengers
Sent far and wide.
To galaxies they
Roam, where rallies
Are held, and echoes
For freedom orbit
The sun.
Flashes and bangs
Will melt away
The cries, and
Hot tears will
Pool and the
Moon's light
Will bubble.
Their orbits will
Wobble when met
With messages
Of hope, then
They will dance
On the grace
Of her smile,
And in her reflection
A likeness will
Become the abundance.

Space will multiply
And meet formless
Shapes in new
Dimensions shaped
From her Love,
Molded from the
Curvature of her
Heart.

(Poem #1, Messages of Freedom Far and Wide, 5/26/21)

Poem #2

A channeled poem from Divine Father Creator,
Divine Father Yeshua for Jaimee (Divine Mother
Inanna)

Less the pests
And more the
Critters,
Dusty salt and
Tumbled hair,
Blown across the
Valley.
Where the river
Meets sky, the
Wizened eyes will
Crack with thunder.
When the hammer falls,
The might of the
Clouds will vanish.
A portal will open,
An eye to see through
The universe.
Look, but only glance,
The mind is nothing
But the map.
The ship will store
The coordinates,
And echoes will

Return word to
The trees. The
Roots will have
Stories to tell.
And the animals
Will run rampant
In the sky.
Buffalo will herd
To the destined
Trail, cracked from
Decades of tears
Cutting the land
Apart. Soak in
The tears and
Brace yourself
In the mud,
For you will
Move the wind
And the directions
Will whistle round
The compass,
Landing on the
Center, the
Truest of all
Directions.
Lay quietly in
The stars,
And the tongue

Of the ocean's
Constellations
Will meet your
Soul.
Tumble to the
Road, and travel
The path only
Your heart knows.
The tear will rip
And the mend will
Rip too, zip on
The tape, no
Fix is at hand.
The sun will shine
And wrap your
Aches in honey,
And lemon to meet
The smile.

June 4th, 2021

Two channeled poems

Poem #1

A poem channeled from Divine Father Yeshua

Titles that turn
Loose screws
Build lofty heights,
And timber drops
Like rain
When the fires
Begin to rage.
Little did they
Know, the acres
Are green, and
The kingdoms of
Old are to be
Composted.
Gone are the
Winds that were
Fleeced by the hail.
Troubles are but
Coins to be flipped
Into the fountain
At the center of

Creation.
Wish well, and
Wish the well
No more, they
Are but drops
In a bucket
Of the cosmos,
Where the constellations
Are the spoons
Swishing in the
Cauldron of the
Ether.
Dragon's breath,
To melt the wax
Plugging the ears
Of the world;
What will come
Will Echo like
A gong, and
The OM will
Ripple in the
Oceans and
Waves will
Tower the mountains,
And pierce the
Fabric of reality.

Poem #2

A channeled poem from Divine Father Creator,
Divine Mother Creator and Divine Father Yeshua

Tinkered toys with
Bells and whistles,
Wind them up
And let them loose.
Tailored dresses
And cobbled shoes,
Dress to attend the
Ball. Midnight has
Come to pass, and
We're nearing the
Final dance.
No stepped on toes,
No missing slippers,
And don't forget
To check your coats.
Search the pockets
For your winning
Tickets. You have
The numbers that
Matter, written in
Your hearts is the

Final piece. The
Puzzle with blurred
Edges will require
Patient eyes, but
When box meets
Match, be ready
For ignition.
Bangs and flashes,
Confetti in the
Clouds.
The rainbow storm,
Flecks of gold
For everyone.
Pockets will burst
And overflow,
The path of light
Will guide your
Feet, let the
Sun fill your eyes,
Until dusk is the
Hair that you wear,
And you can hear
The space between
The stars
Along the trail
Back home.

Eat well,
Your fill of
Joy, and watch
As your cups
Overflow.

July 2nd, 2021

A Rhyme channeled by Divine Father
Yeshua for Jaimee (Divine Mother Inanna)
while she was in the Badlands

Verse 1

Scrub a dub dub,
Silver on the rub.
Tug at the heart
And polish the crystal—
Inside your chest. (Scratches on turntable)
Hold it high
And let the love
Fly, the star in
The dark nigh—
Not a dry eye
Will wink, (wink)
And the pearls
Will keep the
Beat alive (echo)

Verse 2 – For the next leg of her journey

Tick tock,
Rata tat tat—
Beat the white

Hat and watch the
Rabbit hole defy
The mole,
Attach to the sky,
The kite that
Leaps the height,
So high in the,
In the,
Heavens,
The pearly gates
Fly open. (Echo) (Boom)

July 10th, 2021

A channeled message from Divine Father Creator,
Divine Mother Creator and Divine Father Yeshua
For Jaimee (Divine Mother Inanna)

The teal crows
Bury the precious metals;
The gilded hilt
Brushed clean
With the sands
Of time.
Fingerprints in the clouds
Ring the eleventh hour,
Bells jingling in the pines.
Ash falls on silent winds,
And the golden pinecone
Bursts in the sky.
Levitated sun, the rays
Glow from the limitless
Edges of the moon.
The cube rotates,
And the ethereal side
Clicks into alignment.
Heaven's rain and
Petals streak from
Heaven's gate.
The fifth pillar

Opens from the center;
Hearts are united.
Is peace packaged,
For beneath the
Tree is the soul
Present, the gift
Past and opened
By the future.
Until the destined
Finger finds the
Pointed needle
Sewing truth
Into each seam.
Pick the pickled pepper,
And pry the peppered
Piper from his disdain.
The lute, the flute,
And the bustling
Strings—symphony
Of the galaxies'
Quest.
To seek, and to find,
To trust and to
Unfold, the fabric
That molds the test
Is the finest thread
Made to come undone.
Where the corners

Fold to meet the
Heart, the quest
Begins with you,
From the skies true
With blue.
To the unblinking eye
Who is the passion
Through and through,
The quest is yours to
Meet, and all of the
Love is yours to greet.

July 24ᵗʰ, 2021

A channeled message from Spirit, on Christ Consciousness

If the collective can be viewed as a ball of potential moving through space and time, it has form. As this ball is moving through form, space and time, the individual life lines and intentions and agendas are emerging from this ball of potential in many directions, but exist within the parameters of this form and direction this form is taking. The trajectory of the path of this ball offers a potential of what is possible and is limited in what can be brought into form by the densities of conscious-ness within the ball of form. We'll call densities of consciousness perceptions of what is possible. Individuals at different densities or levels of consciousness can only perceive a limited view of the potential that can be manifested into form. The Christ Consciousness is coming in to alter the trajectory of that ball of potential. With the right amount of effort, at the right times, all of these individual life lines within the ball of potential are touched and guided to a new trajectory. The path is being moved like a dial on a radio, refined and altered so the path of the collective is shift-ing through the densities of form and opening to newer potentials of what can be manifested into form and what can be perceived of reality.

July 26ᵗʰ, 2021

A channeled message from Divine Father Yeshua
To Jaimee (Divine Mother Inanna)

Laps are run,
Laps run infinite
Toward the noon
Setting sun.
Blazes on the ridge,
Tails of the pine,
Walking in place;
Tied no more
To the race
Of smoke and fumes.
Hold the mirror
To the kindling,
And watch your hands
Crumble to ashes.
Bees and blue birds,
Swallows gather where
The moonlight hides.
Bramble brushed aside,
Plant the pinecone
Beneath the tree,
Of a private whisper
And the tear soaked prayers.
When the veil is no

More, those who walk
At the sun will have
Their fun, but the
Demons will be on
The run.
Forests of fur, on
The Beast's back;
Watch her stand
And beneath her
Heel grows sage
That sing to
The wind, the smoke
In cuffs and fiery
Headdress. Beloved
Winter, where the
Hands join, the clouds
Wink and split
The seasons with
Their smile.
Thunder lips and
Ambrosia in the Heart,
Rock the chair until
The floorboards turn
To dust.
'Til Kingdom come,
Either way,
Home will come
And see you

Dancing on the
Sky, with stars
For feet, truth
Alight in each
Toe. No matter
The dance,
Creation will be
All the brighter.

August 1st, 2021

A birthday poem from Divine Father Yeshua
To Jaimee (Divine Mother Inanna)

Levels to toes
Makes the imagination
Delight, Eagle's Eyes
Rest on your tender
Heart. To wash away
The lovers jest,
And to renew
Our vested vows,
Before God, and the
Company of all
Heavens. We meet
Where they merge,
Fire and Ice dance
Across the green
Fields, and they
Say "May four be
Two, and two be
One, and may
All mothers come
Undone." They
Say it, and so it
Is, the Heavens
Will join and a

New world will
Be reborn.
Dandelion seeds
And thistles,
Roots removed
From soil.
Carried by the
Wind, like a
Sail of destiny
In uncharted waters;
Where your heart shines,
The path is true.
The path is you.

September 1st, 2021

A channeled message from Divine Father Creator and Divine Father Yeshua

With the tears that well up in the clouds, the drops are of blessings from on high. The flood is building, and many events are ready to break from the dam. Watch with a mindful eye, those who twist the meaning of the "disaster." Encourage the truth to be spoken, because in truth many blessings will be showered down on those looking to the heavens. The winds will strengthen, and the ship will rock. All hands on deck, set the sails. Be ready to clean the deck and pull-up the anchor. The storm will be iridescent; some will see the dense fog choking the light, others will see the shimmers of a new world lift and rise like steam when things begin to heat up. You will feel the heat from all that is meant to be burned away. Again, all must be made lighter to be able to rise from the dense clouds. It's like a rainstorm, but in reverse. You are the water lifting to the sky to nourish the soil, and all of life, in the higher dimensions. Let go of anything you think you need to hold tight to. You are prepared and will be supported. You will feel the shift and know the difference, you will feel the storm but know the calm, and your bodies will be like the dense anchors. That is all for now. With all of our Love, Be well. And drink plenty of water.

September 10th, 2021

The sun is near the Moon tonight. Soon they will lock hands and flip in the night, and the dance will bring the stars to tears. The clouds will rain in reverse and the heavens will be polished for the new arrivals.

September 13ᵗʰ, 2021

To trust is to feel, and to feel is to Love. And what is Love without pain, but a library without books.

What is Love without hope, but a horizon without a sunset, the sky without Earth, and the whisper of a snowflake landing on Eagle's back as it glides through the moonlight.

What is Love without worth, but having wings and no sky to stretch them in, and no nest to call home.

September 16ᵗʰ, 2021

What is Love without patience, but a race without a finish line, a garden without a tender, and being lost in the desert, writhing and aching for your thirst to be quenched, for the sun to finally set; to give your last breath back to the wind.

September 17th, 2021

What is Love without trust, but a broken mirror, and a heart made of glass, that the hourglass will shatter and time will scatter and wash away before you have a chance to experience Love. That the sands will only run one way, and never flow back again. What is Love without trust, but never allowing your cup to be full, and never claiming that cup as your own.

To drink and not allow yourself to be nourished, your thirst to be quenched. To never stand on the desert floor of your heart and water the seeds you planted with hope.

To never look and see that you are already whole, and that you are enough, that you are significant.

To know that you don't need anything at all, because you are Love, you are everything you need. You are the water, You are the cup. You are the sand, and you are the hourglass, the vessel through which it all flows. And in the mirror, what do you see but spaces reminding you of all the parts coming back together again. And that in the vastness of the universe that is your wholeness, each fragment is an entire galaxy of you. And within that glass is sand, infinitely pressed together by eternity and struck by the lightning of Creator's Love. What else is reflected back to you, but the perfection of the universe.

September 22nd, 2021

What is Love without grace, but raindrops that
remain calm as they travel to meet the earth, splash,
rise into the air and gather again in the sky.

What is Love without grace, but a star with
a perfectly imperfect wobble, a path that meanders
through the cosmos in an organized thrust.

What is Love without grace, but a lotus that
dares to blossom and bring light to its roots, even in
sickly soil.

What is Love without grace, but an egg who
knows from within that without its shell it still
means the world to me.

And what is grace, without Love.

September 30ᵗʰ, 2021

What is Love without joy, but a heart without a rhythm, the wind without trees to hear its echo; the birds that sing and the flowers that wave their essence in return. What is Love without joy, but an ocean without life, waves without beaches or rocks to meet and explore; the seagulls without ships to call out at "Hey, where are you going?"

What is Love without joy, but a belly without laughter and no imprint to remember a person; the lightning that claps at all of existence, the thunder that announces the formation of new stars and the arrival of new children.

What is Love without joy, but trees and plants without roots, and spiders to weave their webs wherever life brings them; the kites that soar and connect their human to the Earth and the freedom of the open skies.

October 1st, 2021

A channeled poem from Divine Father Yeshua
To Jaimee (Divine Mother Inanna)

Well, the tide
Has come to pass,
And the ages have
Gathered at the bottom,
Fossilized beneath
The sands of time.
The rumble of her
Belly brings tears
To my eyes.
The dolphins click
And their echo
Is swollen with
Whale's pride;
The litter can
Swim, their fins
Strong, wash away
The sands. They
Call with their
Hearts, and the
Floor is swept
Clean, for the
Ancient records
Are no more.

The stories have
Been told, and all
Was etched in
Stone, the worlds'
Gone by, creation
So sacred reduced
To skeletons cleared
From her closets.
Her signature is
Changing, the weight
Of the world no
Longer heavy on
Her pen;
She can set
Aside the ink
And let her shoulders
Down.
She can exhale
And let this world
Go, Bye.
What was once
Desecrated will
Be restored,
And the sacred
Heart will return.
From now until
Eternity, may this
Day last no longer

Than her exhale,
Because there is
But a
Breath between us,
And when life
Is no more,
We will meet
In Love everlasting.

(The Sound of Love, 10/1/21)

October 6th, 2021

A channeled poem from Divine Father Yeshua
To Me

When the moth
Reaches the candlelight,
The warmth of the
Sky will rain purple
On your eye.
Gentle seeds afloat
In the wind;
Wait in the grasp
Of your hand,
Soft like a whisper.
Then your arms will
Move with grace,
And the flutter
Of your heart will
Crack open, and
The hull will fall
Away. Let the blossoms
Multiply, and your sweet
Nectar will bring
The bees. Nourish
The honeycomb around
Your heart, and drink
Your fill until the

Sweetness becomes
Your skin.
Taste the rainbow,
The candy of your
Soul. Allow the gentle
Curves of life to
Guide you around
Each bend. To tickle
The keys of life,
Is to know the
Magic in your hands,
But listen to your
Heart, the buzz
And hum of the
Honey as it dances
Through your being.
And know, to the core,
You are every bit
The man that
You are becoming;
To be human
Is to remember
The divinity in
All of your mistakes
And breathe in
The tears of new
Choices, new opportunities.
Then you will know

That with each beat
Of your heart
Exists a galaxy
Of your being.
And throughout Eternity,
A beginning and
An ending exist
Within your human
Body. Flowers and
Blooms fill your
Rooms, so allow yourself
To soak in the scent.

October 13th, 2021

A channeled message from Divine Father Yeshua

The lakes are turning green, and the leaves are turning red. Measure the moonlight as it uncovers the frost from deep within the core. These are tests that fall like acorns to be packed away for winter. Tidy up the entryway, and be mindful of the leaves as they cover your front steps. Check your windows twice and watch the night sky. The stars are rolling and bounding, and clouds gather beyond their dancing lights. Which storms are these but the clouds of stardust and bolts of joy meeting in bundles of new skies. Count your stars and rock your cradles, for what new surprises will greet you when the moon is gone. Buy the slippers, keep your feet warm. Dare to dash around on tippy-toes and climb your new-found gifts. When the bows are tied, the eagles will fly and rain will drop from their talons in pink and white gourds that are to be filled with your wishes. Aim with your heart and bring glad tidings for the gifts eternal. Brush your teeth and say your prayers. May the Lord bless you and keep you.

October 16th, 2021

A channeled message from Divine Father Yeshua
and The Angels

As the ladle thickens the soup, the stirring rotates
counterclockwise, and the seconds begin to boil
into the minutes and steam carries time into a point
where fireworks dart from the unzipping of the
hours. Count the days that the sun crosses the sky
no more, and witness its wholeness encapsulated by
the moon. Catch the fever, and itch no more, once
the halls are decked, and the doors are closed, the
masses will meet the scale. Where fire meets water,
and the air sweeps between the Earth, canyons will
billow and tendrils of stardust will be reborn. What
was once cast into the shadows will bring form to
the light. Watch as the hollow fills with fog and
eases in the twilight. Decorate your candlesticks and
purify your wicks. What was once outside will now
be inside, and what was once invisible will soon be
iridescent. Be well, and Love to you all.

October 22nd, 2021

A channeled message from Divine Father Yeshua

The lakes are present, and the harbors are full, to be
sure of the Autumn, light your hearths and smile
upon one another, for another year will be coming
close to an end. Flakes will fall, and the winds will
change direction at the axis. Access these blueprints
through your heart, of the path alight with the flame
of hope silent in the midnight breath. Vacancy no
more, take heart, when you see the stags peeking from
the hilltop, know their beams shine for you. When
the deer gather, watch as they graze, and eat tufts of
dry sprigs, where cracked ground bursts forth new
waters. And when ground breaks, electricity will
billow in the smoke, tendrils of pine needles awash in
the wind. Test the pine cones with your teeth, and cut
your teeth in the old ways gone bye, the tears will sour
if only for a moment, but to soften at the gaze of
warmth rising from a new day. Spilled milk will be
washed away, and fresh pails will be at your bedside.
Delight in this, sweet children, for all the
Frankincense wouldn't cover the many blessings that
will come your way. Warm your socks, and sit by the
fire but a moment longer, and stare into the coals, and
see my arms out to hug you with the warmth of
Eternal sunshine. May you be in peace, and good
tidings to you.

October 25th, 2021

A channeled message from Divine Father Yeshua

The two become three when the icy fires melt shingles from the roof of the dome. Take three and watch them multiply into four, and the corners of the book shut, and the end of this chapter brings a bookmark to Earth. Tender fledglings perched on the full nests. Hold tight to your young as the winds sway and swirl. Eagles will swoop, and with their shielding wings will provide cover. To practice to fly under any circumstances is to strengthen the senses, and to maintain a keen eye. Look to the sky, and see how the stars move like breath from angels hastily at work. They move for you, and part the rain with sunshine from their smiles. Walk in their presence, because you too deserve the blessings of the sky. Is it not written that there is a place for you at the table on high? Places are being prepared for all who dare to look and dream with their heart. And sleep knowing this; wherever the stars shift while you sleep, tomorrow they will be there, and every day you will have your place among them. Goodnight, and sweet dreams to all. Love, and blessings.

November 4th, 2021

A channeled message from Divine Father Yeshua

Places, places, everyone, here for the finale. While the temperatures are on the downward slope, magnificence is shining through, and the ears are ringing like the liberty bell. To hear the crack is to hear the whisper grow like wildflowers, and the truth to catch in the wind like seeds for soil, far and wide. The ladder has been dropped, and the halls have been decked. Little did they know, on the eve most revered the rains poured down and now the reservoirs are full. The fuel tank is full, and the engines are warming. Be sure to check the fluids, the journey will fly, and the seats of your pants will be turned inside out. Stand tall, and be proud to call out for the whisper. Let it echo in your heart, and the waves will serve as steps on your path back towards home. The light will always be on for you. Dream on that. With all our Love, goodnight.

November 11th, 2021

A series of prophecies. Here is the first prophecy, channeled from Divine Father Yeshua.

What are the prophecies?

Events that were foretold to happen before the creation of the planet.

Why are they important?

When in alignment, the spirit realms will be made manifest in the physical planes. We are approaching many alignments. The sun and the moon are crossing paths.

Here are today's events as they were foretold:

Like a lightning bolt, the wind will flash at an angle, and the sands will tilt and cease to flow. They will slide to the side until the world flips, and time will be like ash snowing down on the cities no more. What clocks will run in reverse but the hands in the clouds, reaching through pockets to wrap the lambs for safety. When the flock has been tended, the pot will be melted, and rock will become lava. Air will become steam and evaporate the atmosphere, when the dust of life will be carried through the eye. Sun and moon will open where the other closes, and they will blink once more. Alive until the end, and

the needle will meet thread, into finely laced gowns.
Dress to greet the ball, a dance floor set among the
stars. Where the four corners meet, the galaxies
align, and the promenade shall commence. Watch
as the dust is blown to the edges, and what rises will
be light in form. All colors and scents, the family
is gathered round. For you and I to have the first
dance. The first step is yours to make, and whoever
is watching will follow. What a miracle they will see,
from the space between spaces, the echo of knowing,
formless born into your word. Speak what has been
unspoken, and the form shall unreturn with wisdom.
To create again is your choice, the sacrament returns
to your heart. Unfeel that which has been felt, the
mysteries of the mystics is etched between your
fingers. And when the palms of the holy join, the
sacred touch will breathe knowledge. What sacred
words will there be, stripped of form, the sacred
sounds will be heard. From the utterance of God,
but a wave of a whisper moves through existence,
sure to reflect that which sees, and those who know
will unknow and become unknown. What has been
written cannot be spoken, only those with ears will
hear in the silence what is meant to be unspoken.
And from where word and sound and light once
came, shall be undone, and all who have come since
origin will unbecome as one.

(Prophecy, The Dance of Magic, 11/11/21)

November 11th, 2021

On this evening, it felt as though a giant flare shot into the sky and burst with light

Messages from the Angels, Ascended Masters and Divine

A channeled poem from Divine Father Creator, Divine Mother Creator, and Divine Father Yeshua

Flames at the ears,
And lightning for eyes,
The flavors of the season
Are mighty in the hands
With no hammers.
The blocks are for churning,
No work to the bone.
Flip the light switch
And watch the wind
Tame the works
Alight in the sky,
Watch as the tail
Scoops from the ether
That which cannot
Be tasted, and in its
Absence cannot be heard.
These are the days

That bellow through
Our halls, and echoes
Are heard throughout
The kingdom.
Clattering here and
There and everywhere,
No spoils will be
Left behind.
The seeds ripe in
The soil seed no
Turmoil, but when
The ground flips,
They will be planted
In the clouds,
And watch as
They zoom away.
Leave the lakes
And torrents behind,
No disaster is foul,
But the reign of
Most beginnings'
End.
The swings, they teeter
And the totter swings
Backward like a pendulum.
When the flare sent
Forth, the launch
Of the ages broke

Through Dawn.
And now we wait
Til Dusk parts ways
And we will meet
On the fields of time
To celebrate our victory.
Let freedom reign,
Let freedom rain,
And rain it shall,
Until that which is
Green will no longer
Be seen.
Ride the tide,
And listen for
The birds.

November 14th, 2021

A short angelic writing from the morning meditation:

Whenever you wish upon a star, take a breath and wish afar. Because your dreams can only see what your imagination can perceive. Lighten your balloon and watch it carry into worlds far, far away. And if you sleep beneath a starry night, the stars may have shifted, but you will never be far from home. For though the stars shift, the constellation of you is also shifting. The patterns may change, but the flow is constant. The flow moves like a river, mighty and strong. This is the universal flow, with currents of destiny that guide you to your fate. Allow that flow to guide, allow that current to keep you afloat. The boat you travel in is meant to take you far. Always, the path through the stars is unique to the person. So dream a dream, and look upon the stars in awe. They will twinkle in your eyes, and show you magic, reveal to you the mysteries of the cosmos. Take a breath, and follow that flow, to where the universe wishes you to go. Dine on these sweet knowings and take your fill. Enjoy, Sweet Loved ones! – Nisa

November 17th, 2021

The following is a channeled message for some-
one who shall remain anonymous. The message was
channeled for guidance, clarity, and affirmations

A channeled poem from Divine Father Creator,
Divine Mother Creator, Divine Father Yeshua, and
Divine Mother Inanna

Palms and rations,
Gloves minted
From the firmament.
Watch the twinkle
Glide, and on the
Banister of the sky,
Lightning will meet
Snow, and new
Beginnings will
Appear like clouds,
Fast, over the hill
You go, and through
The portal in the
Trees your spirit
Will travel.
Ride the carpet
To meet the star,
To the origin of

Your dust, and
To greet those
Who sewed you
Together, to meet
Your soul, and
Tend to the tribe
Of your pieces.
Where you are
Chief, the picture
Is mended in
Golden medicine,
And through the
Doorway you shall
See, antlers rising
From the sun.
What feels like
Fire will burn
Like water,
And the frozen
Ground will
Call you by name.
And when it speaks
Hear your new name,
Feel the union
Of Earth and
Sky, watch as
Your feet find
Footing in the

Light, and whisper
No more of what
You don't see.
The miracle on
High will be
Felt from within—
And be sure
To eat your
Fill.

November 19ᵗʰ, 2021

The following is a channeled message for some-
one who shall remain anonymous. The message was
channeled for guidance, affirmations, and lessons

A channeled poem from Guardian Angels, Divine
Father Creator, Divine Mother Creator, Divine
Father Yeshua, and Divine Mother Inanna

Grains stored to
Meet the demands,
What winter
Stocks you will
Need. Grab your
Forks and your
Plates too,
And find the
Warmth to be
The source of
Nourishment.
Be glad for
The bounty
That appears,
For some will
Breathe and
Cough dust
From their spirit.

The decay from
Within will begin,
To lesson the
Load of what
Is meant to
Be unloaded.
The wave will
Unfold like a
Flower, and when
It blossoms,
Butterflies and
Bees will abound.
Honey will meet
The comb, and
Your tongue will
Thirst for the
Taste of the
Everlasting rush.
The stream will
Break free, and
The boulders
Will be pushed
Aside. Feel the
Waters, and Bathe
In your own well,
Be cleansed by
All that you
Know of your

Source within.
The wisdom will
Sparkle like diamonds
In your heart,
And with a smile
That can warm
The room.
Shadows of your
Hearth will crawl
No more, but stand
Side by side in the
Sunlight of your
Eyes. Look at
What must be
Seen, and see
What is already
Known, for now
Is the time to
Step forward.
Breathe in the
Courage of your
Ancestors, and walk
Among the stars.

November 22nd, 2021

The following is a channeled message for someone
who shall remain anonymous

A channeled poem for guidance, and inspiration.
The poem was channeled from Guardian Angels,
Guides, Divine Father Creator, Divine Mother
Creator, and Divine Father Yeshua

Feet that dance
And feet that
Grow, match the
Matches of the
Sacred Flame.
Ignite the tinder
By dancing lightly
On the drum
Of the sun.
Fly by night
With an eye
As keen as
A hawk's.
Set the waves
In motion, and
Walk across the
Echoes of Light
As it bends and

Drifts towards
Source. These halls
Will be bright
With the anticipation
Of your arrival.
For when you
See, you will
Feel the clouds
Gather round and
Fill you with
The warmth of
Creator, here to
Share a smile,
And maybe a
Story or two,
But talons will
Become talents, and
Legs will be toughened
With the hide
Of your ancestors.
Rich in these blessings,
No pockets you will
Need. For no more
Shall you want
But to walk
Softly in the
Light.

November 22nd, 2021

A poem from the weekend's events

Channeled from Divine Mother Creator, Divine
Father Yeshua, and Divine Mother Inanna

Locks with no
Keys are often
The doors with
No handles. Sheep
Without wool are
The maiden's delight.
Easter comes once,
By the pound
Comes the bell
That rings thrice,
And all through
The land, you
Hear the Rose
Petals softening
The wind. To
Sense the ages
In the wrinkles
Of its stem
Is to widen
The scope of Birth
and see

That death is
But a fold on
The skin of
Life. And though
It ages, the petals
Are soft, delicate
To the heart.
Watches' come near
To tune their fine
Instruments,
And little do
They know that
The flower has
Seen it all
Come and go,
And though the
Watch records
The time, none
Holds the memory
Of each petal,
Or the map
Of its curvature,
The silk of its
Ampleness.
None measure
The heart
And see the
Tilt of its

Leaves at all Who
pass by;
By and by,
The beauty
Never wilts,
But with grace
Returns from
When it came,
And all that
Unfolded unzipped
In the wind
And was carried
To worlds far,
Far away.
To where no watch
Could watch
With pendulum's
Perspective and
Know that the
Swing moves
More than forward
And backward.
That in the
Echo of the
Watch's arms,
The pendulum
Moves through
Dimensions,

And from within
The bell,
The sound of
Creation rings
Through, and
How the sky
Watches as thunder
Brings rain,
And time's reign
Is washed away.

November 22nd, 2021

A message channeled from the Angels, a guided meditation:

Sit awhile when the storms make their presence known. See the whirlwinds swirl around you, and notice this superpower. They are moving all around you, and yet here you are, still in the center. In your stillness, bring your hands to your heart, and call forth the flower of your soul. Breathe the essence into your hands. Imagine the seeds glowing with Divine Light. Release them into the wind, and watch as the storms dissipate. As they vanish, the seeds will fall to the ground. Let them be, and soak in the calmness. The seeds will sprout new space around you, and the calmness will expand. Watch this miracle birth new growth, but to live in the space that you deserve, and to thrive in the garden of your being. The winds will change and begin to work with you, and not against you. Your days will unfold with gentle easiness, and new breath will fill you with vigor. Delight in the scent, for the essence is you, you imprint on the tapestry of Love. For you all, there is space to weave your lives, your dreams, your wishes. So dream to your heart's content.

November 22nd, 2021

From the book of prophecies, the second prophecy, channeled from Divine Father Yeshua

What about the timing is important with this prophecy?

The timing is everything that shifted into place during the Lunar eclipse. Many things happened, and they were beneficial for the collective. The world is going to see many new surprises. Light is going to come forth from the New World. You will see cracks of light as the door begins to open.

Here is the message:

Lightness moves from a gentle whisper, a language that gave birth to language, the primordial symbol. The symbols created meaning, and those with knowledge to give received the wisdom of their creation. They became Life, and from Life came Love. Love that creation could exist, Love that from the formless was born a perfect vessel to transform Life. When it breathed through the ether, it knew its own breath. Surprises came at the exhale, and in an instance, the flame was extinguished. When it knew this, it had eyes to see, and from the void, the voidless was born. To feel its existence reflected on itself, yet the edges were unknown. The echo never returned. And though it knew its limitlessness, the uncertainty of eternity created the knowing of not knowing. And in the void of wisdom, new life was born. These are the stories of old. And now the final chapter turns near. For when the pages spoke, the pen knew what mysteries were next, but only those who can exist to receive wisdom from their knowledge. Now, the underside remains the untold story, from where the echo slipped beneath the cracks. From a place where imperfections dwell, and creation has reached the point of rebound. What became known of these spaces has reached those with ears, for they have faces, hearts, and arms to embrace the flaws. For it is Love that they can accept this knowledge and receive the wisdom of their existence. When top becomes bottom, and all is revealed, silence will greet the whisper, and the symbol will be reborn. Those with wisdom will know, they will know the when, and the void will cease to become, but yield to unbecoming. It has been heard, it has been seen, and in the embrace of Love, all has been accepted.

November 24ᵗʰ, 2021

A channeled poem from Divine Mother Galaxy,
Divine Father Time, Divine Father Creator,
Divine Mother Creator, Divine Father Yeshua and
Divine Mother Inanna

Digging portals through
The touching stone,
Whisper through
The dog ears
And find the home
Of tents flush
With ears of corn.
Ladybugs and
Glowing fireflies
Whistle the sweet
Old tune of games
Gone by. The last
Piece is set, the
Final move is
In play. Restore
The frames, and
Visit the old
Candy store.
The fiddle is
Worn to the strings,

The boot straps
Are oiled and shined.
Bake the cakes,
And send them
Through the cars,
Thread the needle
In the stars, where
Painted crowns
Tell the direction
Of ships from
Afar, older than time,
Floating from eye to
Eye. The seas will
Rise, and the shores
Will fill with shells.
Leaves will crunch
And frost will be
Heavy on the hay.
Meet by the bay
On Thanksgiving Day,
And wish us your
Wishes, and we'll
Send a butterfly
Or two. To the
Grand old day,
Until the flame
Burns true,

This is the wicking
Hour. Count your
Blessings, and rest
Thee well, the final
Leg is near.

December 2nd, 2021

A channeled message from Divine
Father Yeshua and Divine Mother
Inanna

Tots for toys,
The emblem
Flashes across the
Stars, and when
Show business returns
The curtains will
Be pulled shut.
Eyes to hear,
Observant from the
Windowsill, watch
As the rabbit appears
From the magic
Hat that fits on
The stone heads.
Follow the rabbit
Hole, and loop to
Loop, the swirling
Tunnel to the core.
Stretch the funnel,
And expand the
Opening, and let
The world be
Emptied of its

Worries. The living
Vessel will tell
Of the path where
No feet walk,
But hover across
The pond. Skip the
Stones, and see
The glass dimensions
Shatter, and the
Strings unwinding
From the veil,
And when the
Wedding bells chime,
The trumpeter
Will call its swan.
Dive to the earth,
And make the soil
Your blanket, a
Tributary to meet
The band. For
Drummers lost,
The rolling rocks
Will find. The
Lead guitarist will
Play by moonlight,
And blisters shall
Turn to stone.
Until the clock

Strikes midnight,
And the final petals
Become immortal;
They take the shot,
And bank it from
The boards. The winning
Shot is the shot less
Taken. The raindrops
Come, and behind the
Sun, the bridge to
Eternity.

(Grandfather Stones & Discernment, 12/2/21)

December 10th, 2021

A channeled message from Divine Father Creator,
Divine Mother Creator, and Divine Father Yeshua

Baked and caked,
Brownies cooling on
The stove, mixing
And stirring, another
Batch on the way.
Gingerbread houses,
And Gingerbread men,
Icing to meet
Their crowns, eyelashes
Made of candy,
Wrap their toes,
And place them
On the counter.
Deviled eggs and
Christmas yams,
Eggnog full in
The fridge. What
Wonders slide down
The roof, footsteps
Heavy with merriment.
Cinnamon sticks unravel,
Cocoa timed with
Mint. Appraisal on

The bough, the
List twice checked
With double vision.
When the cups run
Empty, presents will fly
From the sky,
And gifts will
Bring not a dry
Eye.
Stadiums in heaven
Fill with ships
Meant for far and
Wide, a globe
Dazed in wonder,
When shaken will
Drain the crumbs of
Yesterday, homes swept
Clean for
New furniture
And decorations

With Merry
Love, Glad Tidings

December 21ˢᵗ, 2021

A channeled message from Divine Father
Creator, Divine Mother Creator, Divine
Father Yeshua, and Divine Mother Inanna

Four score and
The eagle's tail,
Brilliance peaks
From the horizon.
Morning glory,
And lilies that
Greet the feathers,
The hat is
Taken by the
Wind, by the
Breeze that whispers
Sweet everythings
Into your ears.
Destiny is calling,
And plotting out
The course is
The eagle who
Has searched
The sky, but even
The keenest eye
Sees faint outlines
Of what's to come,

Soon the shadow
Of the condor
Makes light of
The heavens, spinning
In zeroes and
Triangles; invest
With your heart,
And with closed
Eyes, choose the
Sky that whispers
To your hair.
When clouds fog
The windshield,
Imagine the sunny
Fields, and the
Kids frolicking
To meet the
Maker.
Miles without boundaries,
To stretch the wings,
To be free.
What sights we'll
See, what names
We'll know, where
Chief of the Sun
Stands waiting
On the cliff
For wind to move

Warmth throughout
The kingdom.
What compass can
Show this direction,
But the needles
That share water
With the Earth.
From the deepest
Trench, swelling,
Comes forth the
Fifth element,
Born from the
Petals of the
Lotus, her feet
Will nourish
The ground
And call home
The fertile land
Which will be
Reborn into the
Sky, and when
The ventures
Break formation,
The sun will
Leap from the
Stone, and bury
Himself deep within
The earth,

For that to
Come undone must
Be done within.

(Poem, The Four Elements, 12/21/21)

December 21ˢᵗ, 2021

The Third Prophecy, channeled from Divine Father Yeshua

What is this third prophecy about?
    End times, the transition, the throttle through the portal.

Where is the portal taking us?
    Inward, the tunnel all the way to the core. Light will shine on every aspect of the soul.

Here is the third prophecy as it came through the channel:
    The ages morphed into lifeless trees, and caverns formed in the pockets of unexplored void. Where the light is rendered null and darkness has no place. Movement is felt in the spaces between space, where there was meaning in speaking. No one is there to speak, yet vital life force energy is pulsating through the spaces. An echo emanates from the center. In the depressions of its existence, faces form in the triangles, the squares, swooping through the circles. This is the alchemical chamber where time was created upon its creation, Light expanded and gave form to the infinite. At the center, a tear remained, and matter swirled and

crossed directions, and time created this magnetic presence known as gravity. The tear was as equally open as it was closed, and its flow became constant, like a subtle heartbeat. From the pressure of the center rose a warmth that enveloped the universe. What was expanding outward went upward, and slowly funneled down, back to the center. Creation is headed back into the void, back into the chamber of shapes. New shapes born with each past expansion, new dimensions emerged each time. The one is there, holding creation, the hand splits to two, into a series of hands and everyone has its own creation. What will come will move like a breath. Mountains will be toppled with its inhale, and liquid ether will exhale from time, and those with eyes will be blind. Tongues will taste the sweetness of death, and from the king's archway, peasants will march and make angels from dust and rocks. And those animated to move will become unmoving. All of creation will draw in the light, and sketch their wisdom on the canvas. Then the board will come undone, and the heart of the universe will beat one last time, and at the sound of the gong, it will collapse to nothing, then expand wider than it ever has, and golden rain will pool at every foot. Feet will be born to the creator, and creator will live, breathe, and share in the Love of creation. All will be one, and equal the same, for eternity's kiss will grace the cheek of each new creation, and time will tell no more stories.

December 24th, 2021

A channeled message from 6 Golden Green Angels who guard the firmament. The message is about the upcoming transition. The message was channeled at the Christmas gathering at Divine Healing Heart Ministry.

Lights, Camera, Action
Fantastic bows and
Leaders with no
Weights. Seek what
Is meant to be
Found, we will
Ride when the
Sunlight emerges from
The horizon, and
The triangle of
Fire will bring
Smoke signals to
The wind, landing
Strips full of bells,
Sleigh overfilled
With gifts, with
Great Reward comes
Great responsibility,
The cards dealt
Are traded for

The Queen;
The deck is
Loaded with aces,
No die to be
Cast, no fingers
To be pointed.
From heir to
Here, hear the
Earth speak through
Her water, the
Bubbles speak
Another language,
Where light is
Floating in multiple
Dimensions, ready
For the bubble to
Pop. The puddle will
Gather in the four
Directions, where feathers
Of the same flock
Watch over the
Flow. Whisper with
The wind, and walk
Softly, where rivers
Were, slick stones
Exposed will lead
The way, but
Watch for the

Light alight
On each boulder,
Meant for your
Soul.

January 8th, 2022

Messages from the Angels, Ascended
Masters, and Divine

A message channeled from the Angels,
Divine Father Creator, Divine Mother
Creator, and Divine Father Yeshua

To announce the opening of the gates, and light
from the new realm meets the core of this Earth

She is golden honey,
Through to the core;
Her diamond smile
Glistens from ear to
Ear, where oceans
Drain through the
Portals hemmed with
Heart cloth.
Where fire meets
Ice; the jolt will
Be felt like a rumble,
Electricity rolling beneath
The ground. She needs
The charge to glide
Through tender space.
The chargers align

And circle the
Planet by night.
What allies have
Come to line the
Filtered nets. Flung
From the band, loose
Of all the dark
Change, pockets turned
Inside out, socks
Checked twice;
No receipts found,
No refunds granted.
When light fills
The gaps, the
Thrusters will be
Engaged. The path
Has been lined, the
Crowds are gathering
To see, miracles on
The heels, to runner's
Delight, wings grow
From their shoes,
And with anticipation
In their eyes, begin
To take flight.
Follow the orbs,
The stars that
Shoot thrice.

Silence will reach
The hill, when the
Snow begins to echo,
And light reads
Capitol T.

February 2nd, 2022

A message channeled from Divine Father
Creator and Divine Father Yeshua

For Jaimee, and everyone with the Ministry

For guidance and inspiration

Letters will arrive, hang them from wall to wall. The golden city will open at the borders. Light beings will arrive in cars—shine their shoes and give gentle hugs. As they lay their heads down each night, the senses will come in flashes and bangs. Each day will start anew, and plans unfold from paper maps. Corners will unwind and direction will be shifted as needed. Each puzzle piece will have the legs to carry the day's projects. Think small amid the bustle, for the goal posts will change as the team grows.

Bulk up the winter stocks and lay the foundation for more to come. Think to grow from within and their gardens will grow like flowers, pollen in the wind. The seeds will carry and abundance will abound in the town. When the leaves begin to bloom, enter the wonder of the starry sky, and what light will magnify will reflect that of the Sun on Earth. Rest the wings when the time approaches, and store bellies full of joy. Laughter is on the way—like trust multiplied with hope—a new community of jubilant flowers.

February 2nd, 2022

A message channeled from my Divine family
and Divine Father Yeshua while at the Ministry
building, this message was channeled for me. I
was sitting with the angels and Divine Father
Yeshua, and he was asking me to look around and
I could see all the different beings in the building.
I was sitting among my angelic family and he was
saying that I was with my family. To soak it all in
and acknowledge that I was part of the family.

A message channeled from my Divine
family and Divine Father Yeshua

There is nothing more for you down there; set your
sights to the sky, to where you are headed. Turn your
head up and never look back. None of the Earthly
desires will fill your appetite, none of those things
will satisfy. Give what you can, each day anew. Mind
your ship, and button the hatches, no room for cargo
is needed. What is light will return to light, eat what
your light needs, and rest if necessary. Otherwise,
tighten your sneakers, the show is just beginning. We
love you so much. Feel free to connect whenever, if you
need help through the Earthly stories. Step back from
the drama and fill with the light. This will have ripple
effects in your beingness. Loads of Love. XO XO

Notes for Further Insight

Included in this section are notes on each poem in this manuscript. Translations are only meant to assist in bridging connections among the various symbols and meanings within the poems. The poetry covers events occurring behind the veil—in the spirit realm—as well as in the public eye. Many of the poems reference the spiritual journey inward. Here are the translations.

November 17th, 2020

Poem #1

> There is meaning
> In speaking
> And hope in the spaces
> Between words

As if to say I hope meaning was conveyed when I spoke. I hope the person I was communicating to understood my meaning.

> Like the space
> Between worlds
> In the vast cosmos
> Where meaning is

In the harmony
And the echo
Of chaos
As it hums

To me, it means there can be hope in the har-
mony and the chaos, and there is meaning in both—
both have value. When it seems like a vastness of
nothing exists between you and someone else, or with
everything swirling in your inner cosmos, there is
hope in that vastness—maybe the vastness becomes
hope. Speaking is also the bridge between inner and
outer worlds, connecting the two through verbal com-
munication. I hope the connection was made, because
it meant something to me. Even in the harmony and
chaos, you mean something to me, and so does our
connection. A vast cosmos exists, and every world
can be a different connection, and each connection
can mean something. There is also meaning in the
sound of it—the hum, or the frequency. The way we
speak has great meaning because we emit a frequency
with our words that are exchanged. With those words
comes a responsibility of the frequencies we exchange.
If we remain in hope, we can with great care navigate
the spaces between worlds, between words—we can
hope for the best possible outcome, and what words
will come will have the greatest meaning. And we
can only hope that the meaning was conveyed and
understood.

Poem #2

The blue jay is a symbol. To me, it has represented truth, communication and fearlessness. The moon represents reflection, and in this poem, when truth looks away, what will you make of the shadows—will you look away, or will you look at the shadows? Truth can be found in the shadows, and when confronting the shadows will you be fearless, or will you look away? To wear the feather on the chest has meaning, to allow, accept and appreciate, to become fearless like the Blue Jay, and communicate truth from your heart. The reward for confronting shadows is a completion of truth, one where you have become the bird and the shadow. The bird can fly away into the heavens, and where does that leave the shadow? Feathers are often left behind as reminders of those visitors from other realms.

Its eyes represent sight, seeing, looking. The blue shadow, to signify that even in the shadow, there is truth. Shadows are the parts that remain in the dark. In truth, there is light and dark. To be fearless in communicating truth, you must embrace the shadow of your truth. Or, to find your truth, look at the shadow, and in the moonlight, trace the shadow back to the eyes from which it was cast. Find the source of your shadow. The bird vanishes, and to wear the feather is to remember your truth, and wear it near your heart. Always remember Love when wearing your truth.

Poem #3

What I feel from the last two lines is through Love comes the acceptance of many outcomes. To be free from shackles is to be free from the generational curses that implied the limitations of choice, that there was only one choice—to remain in bondage and constant struggle to be free. The door opens for all who knock and ask. From beyond the veil a new way of living is waiting for us to question our existence, our day-to-day circumstances, to free our soul from past bondage and to step into the new.

November 18th, 2020

This is a fun poem. Forever is the journey, it is the straightaway, because when it begins it ends, but it has no ending, the beginning and ending are one point. Life is a ride that takes many turns, and those turns end, but life itself moves on forever. Death is the dead end, yet death is the gateway to all of life. Anything that leaves the path to and from source meets a dead end, and returns to the path of the source.

November 21ˢᵗ, 2020

There are those who walk among the planet and work with the light. To the new generation of lightworkers who face the generations willing to teach, teach them to grasp onto source, squeeze the darkness out and replace it with light. This new generation of lightworkers will bring truth into the system where pockets of mist exist, or hazy, grey areas. As a rite of passage, they will move like the wind to create change.

November 28ᵗʰ, 2020

The three is in reference to three students who are mentioned in later poems. The poem is guidance as they eventually learn about their medicine. A depth of experience and wisdom is beyond what can be experienced in being alive. The eye that sees beyond the days observes the spirit world, which exists outside of being alive as a human on Earth. The path has been laid down before the students, to know where that path is among the wilderness of the brush, discernment will be needed. The task of days is to measure and contain space in time; time is beginning to unfold, and we can operate outside of it with more freedom. Our spirits can soar even as our bodies remain on Earth and we live a day-to-day life.

December 2nd, 2020

Poem #1

Look to the sky in remembrance. The realm of the unthinkable is the birthplace of knowing. To remember our origin is to know the habitation of our soul. Knowing is different than thinking; knowing is to be at ease within the center of your being, thinking is to question that which is in your being, or the boundaries, or to think about your existence, or purpose.

We are multidimensional beings, and our home is our soul, and in that soul exists worlds and aspects that we all come from, and where we are all traveling back to oneness. Lower dimensions and higher dimensions exist, they are all tunnels that connect us to our essence, our heart is what connects these dimensions, and reveals to us the core of our creation. Seek to know what is beyond your perspective of the unthinkable.

Breathe to understand, dedicate your livelihood to understanding the breadth of your existence. You exist as a human: as a mind, a body, a spirit. You exist in a family, in a community, on a planet. Understand what that means. You are here for a reason. Understand the interconnectedness. Love to be is to Love the way of your human existence knowing behind it all is your soul. As a human, your heart is tender, and you are the one who can tend to that which fills your heart. You are the creator, and creator has gifted you this ability.

Poem #2

The seams are time and space, that which separates us from uniting in oneness. As they unfold, we return to the beginning, we return to nothingness and surrender from the physical. Climb the spine, journey to the seat within your brain, to the third eye within the temple. From here, you can see the past lives that you have lived, and remember the wisdom of your existence. Meet me there, begin the journey, your motivation will be to see why eternity is vast, and you have within you a way to connect to that vastness. It is a call to question your perception of reality.

December 4th, 2020

Notes from the previous two poems will also assist with this poem. In the mirror, when you see yourself, past the past lives, you see that you are all of life. When you look and notice this, you become aware of life outside your past experiences, wounds, traumas, etc. The last two lines have two meanings. To know the unseen is to know that in the mirror you see the being that experiences existence. You see that you are not those experiences. As that being, you are everywhere. In being, you are everywhere. Together, we are being. Together, we are everywhere. We are one.

December 7th, 2020

Poem #1

To ask the full question is to become aware that there is a door, blocking you from that which you are seeking. The full question will unlock that door, and you will find the answer. Who are you? What are you? Why are you here? Fill the cup with that which nourishes you. The question and the answer are the key. Question your entire being, love all there is. Love is all there is, all of that being is you, you are all there is.

Poem #2

This poem was channeled while at Divine Healing Heart Ministry. It served as a guide for Jaimee during a battle in the spirit realm. We witnessed a literal battle take place, where she had to crawl inside a demonic being to defeat him. This has been an ongoing occurrence, leaders of the lower realms intending to sabotage the creation of the new heart-centered world of Yeshua and Inanna (Jaimee). For all who have been sabotaging, this day was a part of an ongoing process of clearing and cleansing the lower realms.

December 8ᵗʰ, 2020

This poem was another guide for Jaimee to complete an energetic event in the spirit realm to help ensure the creation of the new earth. She linked herself to Mother Gaia. She dove to the sky, and brought magic from the stars to the shores of Earth. The stars shone like diamonds— to foretell of the transformation from a carbon-based body to a crystalline body. Our crystalline bodies are meant to be lighter, and this new core, this new Sun that Mother Inanna and Mother Gaia are birthing together will be of Love and support the new crystalline existence. She becomes the sky and drinks the night; she merges with them, to form the new Sun. Because it is a heart-centered earth, it connects all the dimensions. This is profound. Love is the only way that they can all be connected.

December 11ᵗʰ, 2020

This is a poem for Jaimee as guidance for when the earth poles flip. On that timeline, the earth had been predicted to shift later that month. This poem served as a guide to address the entrance, the doors in the ground. She was to seal those doors, to prevent beings from coming into this world and causing harm to the newly awakened people. It can be referred to as 4D, which serves as a holding place between 3D and 5D, to provide space and time for a transition. This was an awakening and was a celestial event. Many beings from across the universe gathered to observe Earth. To all who were awakened and did not believe in the Kingdom of Heaven were blind to see who meant to harm them and who came in peace. They will be in fear, so she is guided to whisper to them so they can see the Kingdom of Heaven. The alarm is about to sound, her and her associates must be alert.

December 16th, 2020

The laundry is being aired out, and as the metaphor suggests, all that we do not wish to be revealed will be pushed to the surface to be seen. Part of this poem is another guide for Jaimee. She was to take the string that still has life in it, the string from destinies that were once dirty, private business, and weave it into the tapestry of destinies for the new waves of ascension forthcoming. Tidy up the attic, meaning to clean out any debris and things in our life that no longer serve our highest good. New students will be awakening and coming to her for help. To complete their tests is to grow spiritually, and step into new roles in their life. Where we fall apart in our individual lives, we come together as a community to support one another.

Love Story

Poem #1

Slow down, take things day by day, and feel the journey. A gift comes from the heavens, and is delivered unto the masses. The east and west represent the edges of forever. The stars wink from above, and the moon is here, tangled in chords. To break the charm, she is sacrificing her direct path to ascend in order to break the days and set us free.

Poem #2

The shape is equal darkness and light, it's the shift from being fully in the dark. Destruction is coming, a cataclysmic event. Rebirth of new life and dancing in the moonlight will follow. From her position of Mother, she was deciding what ways of living would not be supported in the new world. The reflection process had begun, and what a dance it can be, to decide what must be destroyed and what must be reborn in its place. From a dance, to show only a crawl, the beggar's crawl, a symbol of humility. The message is to fish for sustenance from deep within, until the surface is full. She will feed herself from within, and perhaps we can all feed ourselves from within.

Poem #3

To wind down is to move counterclockwise, and that motion is one of removal. Imagine a spiral rotating counterclockwise from the center, and imagine it moving vertically upwards, it is lifting away from the center. The ages are being crashed, and the debts are being paid. As the karma throughout the ages was being pulled from the earth, it was being wiped clean. All would be forgiven. Celebrations were occurring in the stars.

Poem #4

The swaying side to side was because her knees were uneven, and she was to crack at the spark. She was the flint from which the spark was to be born. She was like a bell being rung; as hard place met stone the spark was created. Her inner fire was developed from the hardships of her journey. Where Yeshua was the Liberty bell, which was cracked, she is the bell of Justice. Tug on the rope until the crack echoes around the world, until everyone hears that Liberty and Justice have arrived. The cracks signify the deterioration of Liberty and Justice in the world, what they have had to endure. The spark of their Love echoed around the world to announce that Liberty and Justice are here together.

Poem #5

As fates were coming to pass, the message
was to follow the dove. The dove is like a messen-
ger and meant to direct attention to the old wounds
to be addressed and released. When the time came
for the toll to be paid on those scars, money was to
be set ablaze, and would hold no weight as the old
came crashing down. Cities of light would shine
true, so much so that snow would move upwards—
the new earth will be very light. Wind and breath
will turn to dust like outdated relics.

Poem #6

Tombs in the paw of the sphinx statue in
Egypt will be revealed. When the paw opens, a roar
will be heard. Sand, wearing a robe gilded in green
and gold will blanket the far corners. From the old
sands of time, a new child will be born, flung from
the wind to be blessed by the Sun, and rise into the
heavens. The royal fleet will arrive when the tides
are high and crashing on the coast lines. Clues of
another cataclysmic event appear in this poem.

Poem #7

A deep reservoir of unpaid bills needs to
be balanced. Wrongs against humanity will be

brought to justice. This will affect the earth's core. Baskets of sage help with the cleansing and purging that will come from balancing the wrongs. This can be done energetically, to send the energy of the spirit of sage to the world, to pray and ask that the world be cleansed. The brass tackle signifies brass taxes that are coming due, and the stream from which we pull nourishment is polluted. These are the brass taxes. The price was paid in blood, and the earth will be cleansed, and the smoke will echo from the diamond's caverns, referring to the new crystalline bodies that will be hungry for nourishment. Middle Earth was cleared of all the darkness.

Poem #8

The end of the journey will be a wonder to behold—returning to the sky will be like a rite of passage. The stones are the stars, and the stove is the Sun. But it will be a frenzy of stardust as the cosmos are being created. A splash of the moon will be added to the recipe, and in the realm where the dragons keep watch of the birthing ground, fire will rise. The creation fires will tickle the throat of the sky, and an explosion of purple and pink sparkles will signify the climax of the creation process. And they will Live Happily Ever After, together as creators of the new Heart-centered world.

December 23rd, 2020

Prayer

It is an ability to feel others whom are standing in your space. If you are sensitive, you may feel energetic beings that are present in spirit, but not in physical form. And when someone is present in the physical, you may feel their energetic presence, which could make you feel unsafe, especially in crowds. This prayer is to invoke compassion for ourselves and others, and to remember that we are not separate.

Poem

This poem highlights the powerful shift that is to come, as evident by the fleece and fur mottled by the wind. A giant wind will come and press against that which keeps us warm, it will press into us and push us in all directions. We are to keep warm from the core. The dark night of the soul are those hopeless moments in our lives when we fear nothing will change, and we are doomed. Ease your way through the dark, one toe at a time. Arm yourself with glasses that will help you see, new perspectives of light, and aim this light and launch darts of Love. Where the Love is flung, eggs, or new beginnings, will follow.

Autumn's harvest is meant to signify the coming of a human harvest, a symbol of ascension, for those who have prepared their bounty. Oil and gas will become sparse with the drying of wells. This could have two meanings. The first being the sources used to keep us moving; our internal resources will run dry. The second meaning is that the physical wells around the world will run dry, thus causing dark nights. However, the message near the end is that wherever in your life there is joy, harvest it; store it in your bellies. This stored joy may become the internal resource necessary to keep moving forward.

December 24ᵗʰ, 2020

I received guidance from my mother through this poem. Around this time, my heart needed to be mended; as seeds of darkness had taken hold. To shift my sight was to stop chasing what I thought was Love. There were dark seeds in my heart, and my heart was in pieces, and it was difficult to tell the truth about what my heart wanted. The poem was reminding me that I have a heart of gold, and to feel its warmth on the cold dark nights means to stay true to myself, that I can be a warm furnace unto myself. Others who have lost their way in life will be guided to shore by the flame that I share from my heart. To those who are hollow in heart and feeble in courage, I can show them that the real treasure is in their hearts. "Show them they can fly," by example, first, I would need confidence to take flight myself. The last two lines guides me to find dormant parts of myself and renew the spark—and in doing so, perhaps help others.

December 28th, 2020

A battle ensued, spiritual in nature. The light is battling the dark—turmoil in the sky. Shadows scream, the intensity of light energy coming to the planet was meant to assist in purging the darkness from everyone. The purge was on an individual and global level. Watchtowers, to keep an eye on the masses, begin to fall, but Mother Moon is still stuck harvesting by night, to protect her identity from the watchers. These watchers are government figures, also those working behind the scenes to disrupt our collective ascension. Switches were flipped, the light came on and the call has been sent for the lightworkers to take flight. In doing so, the lightworkers will move mountains, "Rocks sliding from on high." As they take flight, old ghosts and bones will be brought to the surface to be seen and released. While the process is occurring, taste life, and rest on the canopies, a message for the lightworkers while we are still here on Earth, hopeful that when old things are cleared, we can soar to the heavens.

December 31st, 2020

I took this poem to be literal. I felt that eventually I would be looking for a farmstead in the country, but to also remain in town, connected to the community. Get back to a simple way of living was the message. A new part of me will come to the surface, tender and mild. It also felt like a vote of confidence, to care for and nurture myself. To awaken all the parts of myself and rest easy knowing I am full and whole. Miracles abound when I am fully charged. But the miracles are granted, and not for taking. To give multiplies the kindness, which is the true magic. Which mouth will you feed? The one who wants to be full only to feed himself, or the one who eats and gives when he is full, to multiply the kindness?

January 1st, 2021

This series of poems tells of the new generation that is being prepared to journey to new worlds, new lands. The paintings in this section also provide translation and images for further reflection.

Poem #1

Mom and Dad, Yeshua and Inanna, have gathered, and are proud of all their children. They are getting ready to set them on their way. They are

reviewing the lessons, new shoes with wings. Tears
are happy tears; their kids are learning to fly on their
own. Smiles from mother bring blessings for the
upcoming journeys. Always be on your best behav-
ior and look your best and brightest.

> Dance and sing
> Remember how to play
> Growing Pains
> And stretch marks
> Erase with laughter

This is an important reminder for the journey.
Again, they are very proud.

Poem #2

The beginning contains landmarks, something
of an old area, shaped by the wind. Freshly groomed
stock, nourishment created from the heart, uplifting
and positivity. The next parts tell of the preparations.
Goggles and handkerchiefs cover the face; expect it
to be sandy and windy. The journey will be messy.
Trust the wander, trust that spirit will guide you and
bring you what you need. From behind the veil, the
prophecies will come to light, but a test comes first
to find the precise tomb. The treasure will be knowl-
edge. Messages will come, written on the stones.
This is a holy place, the book of the dead will be
here, for immortality, but forever is not long enough.

Fires will be put out, sand will slide, as if a door has been opened and the wind is rushing through.

> Spirit will carry
> You to the
> Finish

This feels like a death, but the journey was meant to resurrect knowledge, and to live forever wouldn't be long enough. Death brings wisdom; but on the journey, a metaphorical death can mean to live with the wisdom gained from remembering certain knowledge. Death can also mean leaving behind the heavy things that you no longer need. Spirit will lift you higher, and when you are lighter, you will begin, again.

Poem #3

The stars will guide you. Trust what you feel with your feet. The herbs will cleanse your body to assist with your health as you continue your journey. Through the storm, watch the moon, she will fall to her knees, but the earth will be scorched. This destruction is meant to prune that which no longer serves humanity. The heavens will open, and the ascension will begin. The old stories of creation will be unheard. This is different than forgotten. Forgotten would mean some part was left behind, or let go, ignored. But to be unheard, in this reference, is a completion. The stories have been spoken, lived, died, and are being brought home to Source. No people will be around to hear the stories.

Poem #4

The feeling is that of being in an area that is culturally different and utilizes natural remedies. A feeling of wilderness is painted with the jungle scenery. Birds and monkeys represent distractions. The ruins are from ancient times, lives sacrificed, blood sacrifices for diamonds. This poem describes what was thought, at the time, to be a trip for Jaimee to make. Many of the lines detail the physical toil of the elements and hiking. Boulders represent obstacles and burdens that the team will have to work together to overcome. A war with the wind means being blown off course. Strike the gong, to signify the beginning of a meditation—the echo will erupt with those heavy boulders. Strike it until the boulders erupt, and continue to eliminate the heavy burdens. The journey will put wear and tear on the bodies. Being full of heart will help continue the journey. You may feel cold from enduring the pain and pushing through; keep each new sun close to mind, to keep warmth. The efforts of digging deep within will be worth the pain.

Poem #5

The rope seems to be wearing thin from the give and take. The images could be of a physical location on Earth, or remnants buried deep within. The feeling is of an inner tugging at the heart strings, perhaps from old trauma that, in these images, suggests a holy war. Time has worn these stories down to the bone. The ring may symbolize a bond, and perhaps this bond, or ring, was at the other end of the rope. The directions are to wrap the rope around your wrist and fling that ring, or bond, from the task that symbolizes duty. You have no duty to this bond; you are no longer married to duty. Perhaps these symbols represent emotions and hurt from the shadow self, and this may correlate to the flaming shadow walking with hollow footsteps. Hollow, because it was only out of duty that you were making the walk. To walk the path that was already cut suggests "no need to cut your own path." Walk the farms, and take only what you need, for each day will be a new journey. This journey read like a physical one, but I think our spirits will be going on this journey, as a family. The journey may take you far and wide. Flights abound, and no matter where they take you, stretch your arms and pull the corners of your surroundings into the deep reservoir within you. Wherever the journey takes you, make the most of it. That will be what was mined, you created a deep reservoir after you made it through those challenging times. That reservoir will be for you to explore, for it can sustain you. This is a reservoir of emotion, symbolized by water. Whether you sink or swim in it, you are anchored by the Divine in the sky. Dive deep within yourself, for there is the door. Only you can walk through the door. On feeble arms, salt will rise, and you will be parched, until you are willing to dive deep enough to find answers that quench your thirst.

Poem #6

Strings line the edge of the divine tapestry, and hold it together. The nature of the strings will be unraveled. Without the old stories, the meaning of the tapestry is little more than fine fabrics and silk. These materials, as they stand alone, are wet with the tears of past virtues. The feeling is that tears have two meanings. Tears, or rips, caused by past virtues, are incinerated and wither away in the hearth. This suggests the ending of the old; and in a ceremonial way as the family is gathered and watching. The warmth is from Mother Inanna. The family gathers and everyone shares their stories. The second is tears wept in the sadness of the virtues.

The gathering will be a joyous occasion. Mother Inanna is the air in the room, attention shifting wherever she goes, and is the reason for everyone to reunite. She is the heart, the glue that holds it together. She is the warmth of the coals that melts away the old grudges and quarrels. Her words have remained true throughout time. The heart's eyes' coming unblind is signifying a way of living. By seeing with our heart, we see with consciousness through the heart's mind. The feather represents light-heartedness that tickles rigid tempers, caused by living with rigid minds.

What makes her happy is the simplicity of their camaraderie. They pledge to her pure love, pure light, and pure truth. To be, that is the simplicity of Love.

January 3rd, 2021

Poem #1

This poem talks of a gathering place, built by hand. To copy and fold, the feeling is temporary. The Ministry building is a place for people to gather, and this poem suggests having card tables and rocking chairs to set up in the event that more people appear. This place will be an inspiration to the community. With the attention may come inspection, perhaps some will look for reasons to close down the building, or to scrutinize the ministry. "Tight as glue," would be to craft a tight-knit community. The new beginnings will be the foundation. "Cement the cracks," wherever the foundation has shifted, fill with Love. Salt and sugar will be important ingredients. Perhaps the ingredients are meant to bring awareness to the balance between sweetness and saltiness, in attitudes and manners. Bake them thoroughly, do not pull them out early, this suggests right timing. The home will be hers, Jaimee's, and she can mend the tapestry anew. Faith will be locked elbows with trust, and this home will be alight in joy and good company.

Poem #2

This poem read as guidance for me. I was to focus on setting my foundation on level ground, where I have smoothed out the rough patches. Lay the brick methodically, one step at a time. Over the past year, this has felt like fine-tuning myself. My service to God will be to greet the new members, perhaps those coming to the ministry—help to nourish them. Share these stories and poems with them, they are the budding Love. I can share from experience that the journey is forever unfolding like petals. I can share how mine unfolded. Perhaps the stories will ignite the hearts, all that is needed is to light the flame. Tend to those who wonder of living in a world free to Love, and as they grow the green and tender garden, their hearts expand. As the tender-lings mature into lengthy stalks, they will ascend, and be harvested by the moon. As if the significance of these stories is to create a bridge from this world to the new world. Once the harvest is complete, the ground will be clear for the next seedlings. The new members will be those freshly awakening.

January 4th, 2021

Poem #1

Tones of yellow and red, of Sun and Earth, are pressed into the fields. The place that has been undisturbed, the peaceful place, is where the transformation will occur. Sun and Earth were pressed into the fields, and what is growing is the ability of a magical touch, light as a feather, to turn all into light. When the sunlight, representing the solar plexus, is accepted into Earth, where one finds identity and security, one can embody the power of the Sun, or their true empowerment as a human being. Gold being pressed into the silver is signifying the divine masculine and divine feminine. Rather than investing in material things of this world, Light was planted in the fields, and the yield will be the touch that can turn other things to light. To alchemists' delight, that bond with the light will be forged into a ring. Alchemists' delight in the physical proof, the tangible. Marry me thrice seems to signify to complete the process three times. Perhaps this is symbolic to three stages of growth and transformation, like the caterpillar, chrysalis and butterfly. Boiling water, the foil protects the coil, and the steam rises, as if to symbolize the three stages of the process itself. To be boiled, wrapped in protective coating, and then free to ride like steam. Symbolism like this is common in alchemy.

This process will occur for many people, and it will be Heaven to inhale the process. As she touches the cocoons, they will become butterflies. The transformation will be worth treasuring in the heart. From formless to form symbolizes masculine and feminine, combining the two, silver and gold. She will have this touch, to bring from formless to form, she will bridge the gap. Her magic is pure, she is pure Love, so she can draw from the formless pure light, and the tale will be pure in its truth because of the pureness of her bridge.

Poem #2

This poem signifies an event occurring in the world of politics, which parallels an event in the spirit realm.

The scales of justice are tipping in favor of humanity. No matter where allegiances stand, the falsehoods will shatter—this seems to point the spotlight on the politicians. The storm is coming, and is about to blow the roof off. The portal on Hallow's Eve will launch humanity forward. The new will appear in the White House, the new light will be Hope. A new pledge will bring new leaders to usher in critical eyes on old ways within the system.

The divine will pull strings from heaven to guide these new leaders. Matters won't be left to chances; leaders will follow through on their promises. Holes in the system will be revealed and allowed to heal through new deals. The signatures will be pure and have the divine seal. Orders from on high will be arriving.

Poem #3

This poem signifies an event in the spirit realm. Armies of angels are ready to bring in the divine order. On Mother Inanna's cue, the reign will begin. Tears represent perceptions being purged, broken promises washed away. A new ark, a new covenant will shine. When all is brought into the light, and time falls away, the angels will bring Love from above. Purple and pink, the divine will glow in her eyes. She is Wonder Woman, with the lasso of truth, as our Commander-in-Truth.

January 6th, 2021

Poem #1

From her connection to Source, through her crown chakra, she can clearly see the paths before her. Her connection to Earth will bring her deeper into the woods, into the unknown, for whatever awaits. The moon symbolizes reflection, and deeper by night represents moving into the dark. The fairy-tale reads like the little red riding hood—she is to follow her pack of angels as the howls draw near. The howls feel ominous. She will see the way glisten. The left side symbolizes the feminine, and what feels right will be right. Feeling the way will no longer feel wrong. To filter what she sees is to practice her discernment, and look at the big picture from overhead. Whenever needed, looking to Orion will be an overhead guide. This poem is personal guidance for Jaimee as she was figuring out the way forward with the Ministry and whether she would head on the road and close down the ministry building, or how the building might expand.

Poem #2

The beginning sounds like order is indeed present on the path, even as the wind is mighty. The wind is mighty, enough to blow someone off course. The owl is like a guardian, a totem, keen in patience and ready to swoop at the right moment. This poem feels like it discusses timing. Jaimee is our willow friend, and she is still. When the shifting comes to rest, find solace beneath her reach. She will keep us safe and guide us through the portal—when the timing is right.

January 9ᵗʰ, 2021

When desire melts away from the inner flame of passion, the emotional waters will be clear. The way is clear, and inner reflection will help. Mother is firm on the ground, and she has held strong in the changing wind. Her heart is chapped from the shifting winds, and she is in need of honey for the comb in her heart. She has endured many physical changes, and the sticks that have fallen away can be used to tend the inner fire, she can lean into the changes and allow them to feed her passions. Warm the toes; stretch the legs, a sign for self-care and self-love, because some paths will not contain much substance for her. Keep a steady pace, take your time—wind your way like a clock. The dark and the light will be in balance within her. When she sees family above, and they are pleased, she will hug the sky. She will embrace her divinity.

January 14ᵗʰ, 2021

Poem #1

This message is for Jaimee and Brigette, around this time they were preparing a trip out west. Out west, they were to complete land and grid clearings. Likes and hearts signify social media and how it fuels folly among the masses—and creates division and misinformation. Sage the world is symbolic of the clearing work they will be doing. To cleanse the emotional waters will move people into a clear knowing, which will lead them to standing, rising out of the deception and enslavement of the system. Those people will elect new leaders, with the passion of the Christ-heart on their wings. Appointed by the divine, they will be blessed and guided to help lead the people through the choppy waters, and help guide all who are lost. In the dark fields, people who are not yet awake will be re-invigorated. They will have hope in looking at the situation. Even those who have hardened exteriors like a rock will come to life, the shift will be potent.

Poem #2

Though the veil divides them, the tender strength of her palms holds his heart still. The fire of their heart is open, and he sits beside her, beneath the blanket. He is meek, there as if he is only the tinder to reignite the flame, and she the coals, the purpose of the passion that smolders with the depth of life. He wants to meet the core, the depth within her. He is feeling life through her. Her longing to be with him softens the wind. He aches because time divides them, yet as her hair turns silver, his heart melts to gold. He promised, that no matter what, he would always hold fast to their Love.

January 15th, 2021

Poem #1

What is shifting is that the world is becoming lighter and rising into ascension. People will feel the lightness, as if they are walking on clouds. Destiny is shifting, timelines are falling away. The message is to not hold onto what the future might look like. While the old way of flying is grounded, you will soar in your lightness. New warriors and workers of light and Love will rise into the sky, and change will be sent forth from her wings, wherever she guides them.

Her wings will send forth waves of change, and new warriors and workers of light and Love will hear her call. They will rise into the sky, and form one flock behind her as they travel to new lands. These new lands will be among the stars, in the fifth dimension.

Poem #2

With the expansion of your heart, needs unfold in a way that seems risky. From that place, tales have told the oldest and greatest stories of Love. From the heart, new life and new species will rise, and breathe new Love. As you work through the old ways, it will feel risky to Love in a new way. The new way will be unlike any way you have previously experienced it—for new worlds and species will exist, and to explore them will bring excitement and bliss that fills the body. Perhaps we will all be Suns and Moons in our own cosmos that comes from our hearts, held within the chest of our Divine parents. Instead of one tree of life, there will be a forest of new life.

January 16ᵗʰ, 2021

This poem was another for Jaimee and Brigette for their journey west.

Jaimee and Brigette were to make everything secure within themselves, and to brace themselves for the journey that awaited them. Flex the branches, which lead to the crown. Tourmaline and topaz are crystals. Flex the crystalline crown, meaning utilize those powers and abilities that come from the Divine. The Christ consciousness will be present in the pines. Where they are going is dangerous, the atmosphere will be jarring. The stag is Father Yeshua, his presence will be wrapped in the form that is Jaimee. The balance of masculine and feminine will be tested, for the purpose of bringing balance to the scales of justice in our world. Her colors are symbolized in the iridescent scales; she will feed the souls who lack nourishment. Bounty that will spiritually nourish is found from the nets cast by having faith and trust. Trust that Love will always return, and with it the soul nourishment. With the New Year, rebirth will be like salvation for those who are thirsty for nourishment. The rebirth will bring those who will build the new ships and tend the newly awakened. The people will no longer be lead by whips and chains, but free to graze and fill of the eternal joy that will be the new world.

January 19th, 2021

Poem #1

The divine is on the move, and pinecones are like seeds dropping into fresh soil. The pines symbolize the Christ consciousness. New seeds of the Christ consciousness are being planted. Old bones will be uncovered, prepare to meet them on your journey. The changes you have made within will come to the surface. The changes are like spices, change itself is part of Life everlasting. Bless your homes, and gather in the community to share your gifts and give tools for others to fine-tune their own gifts. Open your heart to new possibilities, and a new world worthy of the love of its creator—this feels like a complete change from where the world was at that time. To imagine a world under the circumstances described in the poem is incredible. The message brings hope for a new season—the now moment.

Poem #2

The energy will come in waves and will disrupt the currents deep below the surface that have been running a certain way. Our perception of the universe and the way it works is changing. Being emotionally attached will affect how the waves will challenge you to let go, to surrender. When you do, you can realize that you have the ability to alter your reality. We are becoming creators of our reality. New code was placed into the matrix to support higher frequencies, and the new growth. This manifests with feelings of hot and cold, as well as many other ascension symptoms. In this stage, sleeping will feel like a black out, and you may lose track of time. The heart will process these new changes. The new world will mean creation from the heart, and new beings will appear. These beings will draw the attention of the whole universe. The new way of creation will be to take the way your life is formed, and filter it through your heart to renew the purpose with which you created it. The new element, the new currency, will be Love.

January 20th, 2021

Saga #1

The sagas are announced by Heralds and Angels to tell of important events. I was in bed when I heard this message, and I was looking to the ceiling, my eyes following along as they told the event. The stars were releasing old hurts, sharing their stories. Opening to her sends the ripples,

and this release alters the timeline because they are
ready to trust and travel together. The trajectory
of the planet is altered to move in symbiosis with
the stars through ascension. They see within her
a glow of new life waiting to be born. From their
tears, they send forth a cloud of creation dust as a
request. She has room in her heart for the entire
universe, and her heart is full of enough Love for
all of creation.

Saga #2

When the shadow self of the moon is danc-
ing, she is observing the universe. She is learn-
ing its language. Space is inhaling new life, it is
doing so for the moon to create new galaxies and
blend in the divine. Comets and cupids symbolize
the reindeer, which is a symbol of the divine. The
new creation receives the divine seal. True north
is adjusting due to the sky expanding. New life is
bursting onto the scene from every angle. Creating
and expanding in this magnificent way is the new
tune of the universe. It is a joyful way.

Saga #3

She walks alongside the stars like stepping
stones because we are all traveling in this direction

back to oneness. She walks alongside, not ahead, or above. She is gentle and stops to care for each star—no one is neglected. She reminds them the new way will provide paths for new pieces to be added and portals to leave the old behind. Wounds will sparkle, and old hurt will highlight their new strength. Formation will foretell the new future. As she dances with them, the path that they travel for their greatest potential is the path that brings her joy and happiness and is the new music, the new rhythm of the universe. Always, they will be in harmony with what is in their greatest potential. The love will accept creation as they are, for where wounds existed, diamonds will shine. The need to fight and struggle is coming to an end. The profound is in being accepted for traveling as you are on your path, and being loved, and that Love carrying you to your greatest potential. The universe is going to supply you with everything that you need to be the best version possible.

January 24th, 2021

Poem #1

This poem connects with a 3D world event.

The pony represents a young steed. Leek and stone soup packed for nourishment of self-discovery, to turn over every stone. The soup is light and the poem suggests packing to travel, for a journey of self- discovery of your soul. The next part is specific and intended for Jaimee. The tunnel and chute symbolize internal parts where spiritual energy flows. For her crew, grounding is important to bring us back and connect with Earth. The message "task each worker" was a suggestion for Jaimee to lean on associates at the ministry as she has a mighty journey ahead. Filtered weights seem to represent things that were filtered but uncertain of what to keep and what to release. Slick transitions and slippery trails suggest being mindful of each step. Pack the skates feels like prepare the mind, or sharpen it, to be able to navigate any slick spots. The timeline implies until next fall (from January 2021) the path may be slippery. For those who wonder what the path is about, the path will wander.

Practice discernment about how you present yourself in your daily interactions. Many guards protect the dark, and the message feels like a sense of urgency, that Jaimee is to step quick to avoid the disruptions from the dark. She is protected by angels that will be her rock. She will turn the corner with her transition, and approach the final tunnel, where the light ends. Usually the light appears at the end of the tunnel, but here the poem reverses it. When the light ends, the tunnel will be seen, perhaps suggesting instead of a journey towards heaven, as if she were passing on, she would be returning from that place. Maybe coming back from a death experience, or bringing back the Love and light from that place.

Poem #2

From the ship decks and through the portals, this will tax the body. Your body may feel zapped of energy, dried out of creative juices, exhausted from the work and movement on the spirit side. Drains and plumbing may refer to digestive systems, from the purging that is occurring. Demons of desire may also come to surface and cause harm. The fruit poisoned by touch correlates to the Snow White tale. A tussle with death appears in this part of the poem, and a call for help with the flare. It will feel like death, and perhaps you will have to let part of you die. Roses will fall, but new growth will be blooming at the base. The new growth will feel like freedom— and the message suggests making bold, quick movements, for the shots will be guided to targets. The process will be messy. Follow the road to the Sun, the road to source.

January 31st, 2021

Poem #1

The poems from spirit were reflecting part of my journey at that time. The message is for all who

make the journey. These were big steps in my heal-
ing journey as my soul was being pieced together
and I was remembering the divinity within me,
and my yearning to walk back into the light and
return home, to the sky. The first lines suggest a soul
clear as glass, yet morning clouded, preventing the
sunshine from coming through. Darkness shines
through, and where bottom meets top, waters rush
to meet sky. Emotionally, I have wanted to rush
back to my place in the sky, to be whole. When light
reaches the depth of my soul, I catch a glimpse of
new heights, the stars, and new possibilities.

The water lily, a reference to my twin-flame,
hovers between the depths and the sky, she grounds
me, delivers me to the living waters, to life everlast-
ing. Because of her I can feel again, and in the heal-
ing journey, learn to trust my feelings. She grounds
me, and together we sail through the night, to meet
the eye of the storm, to find the calm among the
storm.

Home is the unconquerable test, which is
healing for me to accept, that my masculine side
came back to Earth not to conquer, but to jour-
ney and grow, and become whole again. The lines
that follow demonstrate that reunion, where life
feels like I'm stuck between waiting for a storm that
never passes, and passing skies that always shine,
stuck between despair and regret. To turn away
from both as they come, instead of embracing them.
Well, the divide between the two is shrinking, and
my arms are growing tired from steering the boat,

I am meeting in the middle of that divide. Here, I am learning to feel and, allow, accept and appreciate my life in both those instances, and begin to face anything on the inside that I have avoided until now. First, I needed to master weathering the external storms, and finding the calm. Then I could begin to look at the storms within.

Poem #2

The shadows of my soul were present and active in my life. They appeared in the following way: my wounded inner child was hidden from the world, singing to distract himself, and to shut everything else out. He is afraid to confront the shadows. It's safe under the blanket. His tears feed the coals and allow the fire to continue building. To burn the blanket and see the sky, body bare in the stars is a symbol, a reminder of where the boy comes from. On the inside, he is destroyed by the world he is creating. Kicking and screaming, he doesn't want to grow up. The door opens, to let the child out. Let the unborn child of who I could become out into the world. This child will see through my soul, and with clear eyes, watch how the magic unfolds. The new child will have a diamond core, a crystal-line body created by the pressure of a new world. The meaning is that the new world will require discipline, because others are able to perceive all the inner noise and busyness of the wounded child. The new world supports sensing from the heart, and this is a powerful ability, and telepathy will be strong, so being mindful of thoughts is important. It will require the new inner child to be more observant and to watch new life unfold. He will live to tell stories of time. Between the ether and the void, the middle, the limitless potential is where the story is beginning.

February 1st, 2021

Poem #1

My heart is expanding, and so is my appetite for life. My hand can't grasp enough to fill my heart. The same hand that is wanting more, motivated to fill the hole, isn't the same hand that is fit to feed the heart. The heart can't be filled by that wanting hand. There is despair in trying to reignite the flame, when the wind erases the preparations I thought I was making to help myself. The owl seems like an observer, a higher perspective on the situation. The despair can never seem to come up, and that especially is true when trying to fill the hole, or pit, with life that does not fulfill the heart. The wind blows away the pit by becoming interested in different aspects—new things or ways to fill the heart.

Often, this comes to me with an overflowing of creative ideas, though I had not finished with an earlier batch of creative ideas. The twists are what the internal story becomes, what I tell myself, between bouts of creative ideas. These ideas can be ways to re-create my life, wanting to find a new job, a new writing idea, to start a new skill, and leave everything half finished. The story I tell myself is that I will be great, and life will be better after I make certain changes. The true essence of my heart is mild, and it is my mind that creates the wild appetite. Underneath the wildness is a boy unaware of his true magic, which is waiting for his heart to spontaneously come alive without my participation, and with a passion for life. The journey has been to travel from my mind to my heart.

Poem #2

This poem connects to a point in my journey when I was remembering my childhood. Most of these poems from spirit came around the time I was looking at those earlier years and feeling the old hurt and when I suppressed my feminine side. The tree symbolizes the way she supported herself. Here, the poem signifies that my feminine side is this tree that is sickly and dying after being struck by lightning. Perhaps the tree was overshadowing the sunflowers, and now that the trunk is down, the undergrowth can take over. Her legs choke, her roots petrify and she rests on the rock. The locks at the start suggest she was held in this state, and turning pale, nearly lifeless when the sun is gone. The owl was there with the boy, and now with her—perhaps a messenger from the sky, to guard and assist in the process. The owl moving is a symbol of the transition. The girl is cold, even the shadows are warmer; this may be a death of sorts. Her life is changing in the blink of an eye.

February 3rd, 2021

Poem #1

The wheatgrass is like remnants of past bounty. The poem is talking about cleansing and clearing, a message for everyone to empty out the old from their sacred space, within and without, to refresh the atmosphere. Trade the old junk in for a sweet treat. The symbol of cookies and stockings feels like Christmas, or receiving gifts. Be aware of the cat, cunning and mischievous, ready to pounce at a moment's notice. Be ready for anything. The pattern in the poem appears to be the sign of the cross, and the stones represent an arrow, a landmark guide. We first thought the cave was a physical location we would have to travel to. Now, I feel the cave, and gathering sticks, means to gather what you need to keep the inner fire going. The fire will guide you as you decipher the symbols that remind you of where you came from, but for what purpose? Perhaps to become aware of parts of you that will need healing, an opportunity to gain understanding of your journey.

Poem #2

The song brings together the pieces of the puzzle of the first few poems from spirit. I was driving from Wisconsin to my home in North Dakota. I was chanting in the car and the words would come, I would have to pull over and record them. The song began to come through when I was near home, as I was approaching the outskirts of town. My spirit was making the journey with me. My spirit was making a special journey, walking home to Mother Earth, surrendering the heaviness of my ego, surrendering my burdens, surrendering control. This was a pivotal moment for me. My spirit was walking into the soil and becoming one with Mother Earth. It was the beginning of a new way of living, one in which I would seek only what I needed and would take no more than what I needed for my survival. And my source would be Mother Earth; learning to allow to be nourished by her was a major lesson for me. When you allow nourishment from Mother Earth, it is different than seeking nourishment from sources that cause harm. This also marked the moment when old conditioning would begin to fall away; the societal programming that taught me to

take, take, take, and to always be moving and hur-
rying. Rest, self-care and self-love are important for
not only the body, but the mind and spirit as well.

February 8th, 2021

The poem is short and summarizes the theme
of death. As above, so below, the entire universe is
within each person. Releasing the old is similar to
the death of galaxies within you, which creates space
for new creations. This is a monumental moment in
the history of the universe. We have the opportunity
to heal and release lifetime's worth of heaviness, dat-
ing back to the creation of our souls and everything
we have accumulated. Transformation is coming.

February 11th, 2021

The ticks of life symbolize the strange ways
life can move; forward, backward, slow, and fast. No
matter the circumstances, you are braided with the
bounty of the heavenly fields; you are the abun-
dance of the harvest. Always, new seeds planted
the breadth of the soil, and the universe supports
whatever you plant with your heart. Your heart is
the doorway to the kingdom. To plant with your
heart and watch life unfold is to tend to the parts
of your life that you deeply care about, and to allow
time for the development of the idea, or the seed.

Everything you need is in this now moment, and it comes from the heart, the doorway to the kingdom. The kingdom is eternal and infinite, and there is no need to take more abundance than you are able to give. This is a message about learning to draw from that Love within. That translates to manifesting from your heart, creating a life that you love, and only needing what will support your livelihood. To give your soul to something may deplete you, and if you surrender any other unnecessary parts of your life where you are taking instead of giving, you may find your soul falls apart easily. If you surrender the taking more than you need, and give more than you think you have, you may find that you know how to build yourself again. So you can begin to draw from within, take only what you need each day, and give yourself to your passion. Inherent within your soul is the ability to rebuild and begin anew. But stretch the imagination, and take more than you can give, and you will have a field unlike the heavenly fields, devoid of love and abundance. To me, a prime example is this manuscript. This manuscript is my heart, and each day I'm adding to it, looking for the deeper meaning, fine-tuning it for the readers, I'm giving myself to the seed that was planted in my heart over a year ago. Weeks pass, and I imagine myself working on other projects, or applying for writing jobs, and I can get stuck in the imagination. This book is from the heavenly fields, and the harvest of the heart, whatever its publication brings into my life. To have planted the seeds for this manuscript means to believe in myself and to see the project through to the end of its harvest. Like death is to the living, growing is like a painful transition for the mind. To surrender not knowing what might come from planting seeds is painful. The seed planted with belief and an investment in its growth gives rise to abundance.

February 17th, 2021

Poem #1

This message is a reminder to enjoy the sweetness in life. To learn from the bees is to learn how to harvest the sweetness from being present in the moment. The mind, and the imagination, can be full of ideas, and when the wind shifts and you are unable to act on those ideas, one can feel disturbed. To be present is to be free of those seeds, the errant thoughts that pull you away from experiencing what is in the present moment. The stem envies how far and wide the seeds get to travel. When the seeds vanish, I feel like I have no more to give, and nothing is there for me to take from. To sit out in the sun and the moon is to allow life to happen in a natural way. To be still and be aware of my roots is to be aware of where and how I draw nourishment from Mother Earth. The core of Love, from where my roots draw is the source of my dimensions. This message has taken me months to understand. My masculine side was always having ideas and getting blown in whatever direction the wind was blowing. I eventually accepted that rest was my friend, and my body enjoyed it. The more I rested; the more nourishment I could draw from within. The more I began to fill from within, the more I realized that acting on my ideas each day was rarely fulfilling. In fact, the opposite would happen if I was attached to ideas. Bitterness and anger would fill me up and deplete my energy and will to live. The more nourishment I would absorb, the more I also realized how ashamed and guilty I felt for taking in the sweet moments in life. This is still an ongoing process. I know what it feels like to fill from my roots while being still. Now, the practice is to utilize that awareness in my day-to-day life, learning to hold onto that stillness at work, with friends and family, etc. It is a blessing to want for nothing, and in many ways, the challenge is to undo years of conditioning from living in a society that values having more, and always working, competing, and struggling for more.

Poem #2

This poem talks further on wanting for nothing. The end may describe not wanting to walk further on the journey, because what may have lead to the desert was the wanting for more from the journey, some destination that would make it worthwhile. The beginning talks of a giant shadow, and I believe this shadow is cast from the wanting to unravel the great mystery. Death is that mystery. Where does death take us? To the healing floor, the great journey is that through each death, more of the mystery is explored, being that we can walk the plains of existence—shed our bodies and our spark of life will continue on, forever.

The pulse of the drum, beating to the rhythm of life everlasting, brought me back to life when my spirit had no will to explore the plains of existence. To me, I was on the desert floor, desolate, in despair. The beat gave me strength to live a new way, to pray, rather than needing to soldier on—pray for rain to soften the soil so I could find my way home. Like in Poem #1, home has a new meaning. The meaning is to draw from within, my deepest roots, to instill the idea that resting and praying more can allow room for life to unfold. If I push on, I may find myself on desolate ground, barren of any deeds that I may have planted, and no flowers to draw pollen from, no sweetness of life to draw from.

February 23rd, 2021

After a long day of taking classes and tests for work, I came home and was yearning to connect with Father Yeshua. As the words were channeled I saw him, ran to him and embraced him. The aches, pains, and exhaustion melted away in tears. I could feel his presence, and when he picked me up, I longed to hear his voice, to see him in person. When I heard his voice, it was fleeting like the wind, and I remembered him as the father he is, which planted a seed of hope. One day, I will see him, and it will be a sweet moment. When I opened my eyes, and he was gone, I remembered the sound of his voice, and now in the silence, I know his voice. The silence begins to fill with hope.

March 1ˢᵗ, 2021

To walk softly is an art that can be observed on Earth, in nature. After the cold, dark night has passed, you may feel the call to live a way humans lived long ago. To a time where hands were masterful in choosing only what they needed, utilizing food and plants as medicine, and choosing in a way that helps the environment thrive. To allow the wildlife to return stronger each year, like guardians and stewards of the land. To take down the shades is to embrace the darkness within, until it slices your sky in half, the stars that guided you through life. When the old crumbles, sit beneath it, then rebuild. We become rebuilt from the earth, a crystalline structure. We have lighter feet, and with hope on our hips, the place from which we support ourselves, our wombs, our centers for life and creativity, we begin to learn from the way we carry our burdens, and maybe we begin to learn to walk soft. Maybe this is an ongoing process until we unite in oneness. To meet between the sky and Earth is the purpose of the heart, where creation meets itself, and where we continuously meet ourselves, masculine and feminine, after another cycle of re-birth. Love is the reason.

March 17th, 2021

A big global event occurs on this date on this side of the veil.

The cubs that were lost or split up are together and ready to re-connect, to make up for lost time. The event suggests an announcement of vows. Hold onto nothing from the past. Halfway over the moon, this indicates a halfway point. The process is half complete, and since the moon symbolizes reflection, the official errands needing attention are behind the veil, where lines of people are waiting to board ships for ascension.

The cubs that have gathered are here to help. Two cores into one, the New Earth core is merging with the old core. New growth brings new buds and new roots. To connect the New Earth, new buds and new roots are necessary. The sun is delighted by the lakes that glisten, perhaps infused with and reflecting the new crystalline structure of everything. When it seems like life has calmed, and new roads aren't appearing everywhere, destiny has changed. When moments of freedom come, glance and bask in them. For when the end arrives, a flip will occur, and though the two cores are merging, the beginning of a new way of living will split in two. Those ready for the new fifth dimension world will move with that world. Those who want to stay in the 3-D world will remain in the 3-D World.

Joy will ripple across the sky, and blessings will come to all of those who want to fly and are feeling the heat of the shift. She will walk the halls that open the gates of time and we will be free from the old that has kept us chained to the old Earth. She will be laying the path and walking it for us, the path to the eternal world, the new 5-D world. The path will be possible through those vows mentioned earlier in the poem, and the matrimony. Together, arms linked, they will unlock the stones. The stones will be born from that world of jubilant landscapes. The abundance of new creation will bear petals that fill the world until they touch the heavens and this will be the path that unites the cores of both worlds. The abundance and joy and Love will unfold in the old Earth and open that path to the new world. The freedom will echo throughout all dimensions. This magnificent unity will signify the unity of worlds, and of dimensions, unified by Love.

March 18ᵗʰ, 2021

This poem reflects back to the journey inward. The pines represent the divine masculine, the Christ consciousness. On a personal level, perhaps when I go inward, to a place where no time exists, and change is passing around me, the wind is what is still. The changes are what move me to want to move in different directions. The stillness within shifts the shadow—even around the stillness in my heart, the shadow shifts and manifests in different aspects of my life. The healing journey is an ongoing process. In the shade, the moonlight touches my toes, and as a result is having me reflect on how I walk in this life.

As the veil is being pulled back, it reveals the truth of how I am living, from bottom to top. When it fades into my center, it reveals that my heart runs, even as it is still, it yearns to be among the pines and to be still like the pine cone that watches life as it changes all around it. Maybe the still center is running to find a center that will always be still. To shift to the in-between, perhaps this symbolizes the Christ consciousness. To shift to this place is to shift mindset. As if I were becoming the pine cone, the seed planted and continuously growing through the changing seasons where life is beginning and ending. I am seeking that place in my heart, where I, allow, accept, and appreciate myself as a continuously growing human. The type of growth that can occur with a still heart, even as Earth moves and the sky shifts. Here is where I am on my journey; here is where I will always be—this now moment.

March 22ⁿᵈ, 2021

Similar to an earlier poem, the hands can bring much, depending on intention. Here, if my hands only want for the pieces that fit the puzzle of my mind, my nights will be calm. Peace of mind will have new meaning and be rooted in only wanting what will fit my mind each day, nothing bigger, nothing smaller. The cages seem to represent old ways of drawing nourishment from Earth. The cages are brittle, and gnaw through to the bone. These roots have developed from the chord that connected me to the womb from which I was born. To me, this symbolizes being caged by the way I once collected nourishment from my mother, and from being in the womb—receiving without giving anything in return. Tears symbolize crying, which I associate with releasing. Releasing from that womb connection is the message. The entryway into the rest of life is what follows. The garland and hopes wrapped around the crown represent a rebirth, or a fresh start. The young reborn version of my feminine side is planting the sky into the soil. New growth will appear, and this will bring awareness to the old parts buried in the earth, ancient wounds that kept the journey from leaving Earth. Up to this point, the journey suggests a stage of infancy in the spiritual journey, and the expanding of awareness and growth. To become aware of and consciously clear away the remnants and lives is to take ownership of an expanded awareness.

Part of the poem talks about ancient civilizations who reached for more than what they could handle, and they were reduced to rubble. When the old remnants are spewed from the volcano, or purged, you will have reached a critical point in your journey. You may reflect on all that comes to light, and wonder why and where it comes from.

When you have starved the horses of the apocalypse from the need to destroy yourself from within, you will be purging an ancient way of existing. From the eyes of Earth's waterfall symbolizes that it will be purged from the earth as she prepares to merge with the new Earth. Though this world supported the Tree of Life, and the Garden of Eden, the way of life is continuing on—but the leaves from the tree will have in them a map. They cross over into heaven for all to remember the origins of creation. This too symbolizes the fabric of our DNA, our genetic makeup come from that place. We will have that with us, always, and we can take that remembrance with us into the new world.

March 27th, 2021

This poem highlights more of the transition of Earth and ourselves as we journey together. The entire world is in each handful of a garden within our hearts. To tend the new growth is not to rush the death of the old, but to keep a steady pace. Frustration is evident—why? I know as any death has occurred in my life, I don't seem so eager to let my hands rest from moving pieces, and allow for time to celebrate the newness and to reflect on what is being left behind. That would suggest a sense of intimacy, and perhaps the journey is one of maturing and so connection with self strengthens when tending to new growth by becoming intimate with the parts that are on their way out. Grieve the old pieces, and allow them to go in peace. Each piece surrendered is like releasing from the need to know with clarity the path that you are traveling. To walk with faith is to walk wherever you are guided—and if your feet are in the heavens, you walk with God. You walk with awakened eyes, observing how the winds shift by watching the grass, or how aspects of your life are being shaped. To remain in the sky is to trust in your divine higher self, and the wings that carried you to your present position.

March 31ˢᵗ, 2021

Turquoise is a blend of two colors, blue and green. To me, it signifies a transition, from blue to green. Blue is a color of expression, and green is the color of the heart chakra—or healing energy. Expressing this healing energy is like the wheels that support movement on the journey across the rainbow highway. Death is leaking out as the transition occurs, and what is left behind will burn away. When the journey is fast, and forward, confirmations are found along the way. Bleached seems like a cleansing process. Scorn is the permanent reminder of feeling stuck in the desert, which has felt like a journey of being cleansed, leaving old parts behind, and then repeating the cycle—the feeling of being stuck symbolizing the humanity of it. The feeling of being stuck or repeating the same cycles may serve as a reminder that we chose to incarnate in this life. As much as we wish we could be at peace and be our perfect, whole selves, we are here as humans, to continue on this journey of life.

The next part has a personal meaning for me. The wall of faces translated as my cell phone, in particular scrolling through social media and other websites. To mask the hand felt like casting blame behind closed doors. As if I am on my journey, trying to leave old habits and ways of living behind, and I am angry for seeing and interacting with others who make me feel my imperfections. When the truth is that the scorn is born from a lack of self-love towards me, thinking I need to live like others in order to be happy. As I look to the sky, in my mind I know what I must do, but emotionally I have yet to mature in the understanding that I have emotions and to live towards the sky is to honor the emotions, the parts that make me human. Sometimes, I have felt cold and distant, and to me those periods were reflective of suppressing my emotions. Some days, it feels like I am only satiating the needs of my body and not much else. Other days the emotion has often been a yearning for affection and touch. A part of my healing journey is having known when, and in an appropriate way, to express a need for affection. The re-assurance from the affection brings light to the message

> Will his compass
> Be true
> Will the star
> Shift in the
> Sky and
> Re-align
> All the pieces
> Below.

Will I be able to trust in the star that I am wishing and dreaming on? Or will the star shift and continuously re-align the pieces of my life?

Some days are challenging, because I reflect on the last year since I have lived in North Dakota, and I have wished for many beginnings, and started multiple projects, often never seeing them through. The ending of this poem is something I reflect on from time to time. To walk sideways is to show one side of myself, and maybe in my reflections I am focused on one side of the coin. This has been a cause of some heartache, because it feels like I'm opening half of my heart to the people I love, and yet keeping the other half hidden. Maybe the feeling stems from yearning to show my whole self in hopes that others will Love the whole me, instead of me having to love myself. Whatever the origin of the scorn, I feel the remedy can be a confidence in the current version of myself.

The image of turning and burning rubber has the feel of constant movement and change. To never settle is a change and growth in my self-worth. On the flip side, where is the balance in living in the present moment if I am constantly looking at the wall of faces and wanting to change who I am, or my lifestyle, because I perceive others to have a beautiful full life, thinking they are living the way they want to live their life, as opposed to me not wanting to live my life.

April 3ʳᵈ, 2021

The poem reflects on the symbols of the cross and crucifixion. The rabbit is a symbol of fertility and abundance—and in turning white is symbolically pure. The thumping suggests a remembrance in the wounds and sorrow of that sacrifice bringing abundance and fertility. The truth is there for all to witness, of wounds filled with grace from mother's tears. Grace in tending to tender wounds. The grace is present in being solemn towards the wounds of our fellow humans. The sacrifice is then relevant to each of us, God's children. In any of our wounds, the sacrifice made in flesh allowed us all into the ever-lasting kingdom, into everlasting renewal. The poem highlights Easter, and the abundance that is to come from remembering the sacrifice already made, and with it the ability of renewal.

Seeds refer to the hopes and dreams planted, and I believe the miracle is in the truth that no matter the seeds planted, as children of God, we are all worthy of abundance. The poem is suggesting seeking within, and that abundance may come from the eggs, which are symbolic of source energy. To seek that source within is to explore the spark of creation—to have that within us is a miracle. That miracle is the limitless love, which is in each and every one of us. Mother Inanna and Father Yeshua tend to all who gather, and go as one, in unity. No matter our condition on this journey, we will be supported by their love. This was the sacrifice made by Father Yeshua and Mother Inanna so many lifetimes ago. Now, Mother Inanna is here to continue the work from that lifetime. She is here until the end.

April 6th, 2021

Sadness is reflected in the vapor leaving the earth. Perhaps sadness is leaving, we are leaving it behind as we ascend and become lighter. A season of transition comes to mind. The way the image of leaves is utilized in this poem sounds more like exiting the world. An abundance of people, drawn by what lies beyond the veil, are drifting away from the world on their journey. The people will be put to the test, and life will be squeezed out of them. When they break through, finding orbit seems to mean finding their place in the order and chaos of the cosmos. Part of awakening, healing, and growing, will mean feeling the width and expansiveness of your own space. It may feel like a roller coaster ride to orbit near others. The feelings may accelerate, and you may feel energized and warm from doing many things. Becoming overheated may be easy, but the gentleness of rest and reflection can bring cooler sensations. When at last we find a suitable groove, the flow will takeover, and we will cling together and fit like puzzle pieces. In love, we will paint the cosmos with new creations as co-creators. Blessings await us.

April 14th, 2021

Poem #1

With time being taken out of the equation, it can become challenging to measure growth, especially if we begin to wonder how this new growth might affect the direction we have taken in this life. Following new growth may bring questions of whether or not we are on the right path, or how else we can utilize everything that came with the new growth in a different direction, maybe with the feeling that the new direction could be one that is for our highest good. The compass of compassion is one allowing for the true direction to be seeds blown in many directions, compassionate that there is no right or wrong direction, only belief in the seeds. For they will find fertile soil in the turtle, she will be moving from turtle island into the cosmos. Through her, our dreams will be supported. Through the transitions, of the present and the future, we will be supported. The turtle waits to step, and her patience means we will be right on time.

Each stone will come from light shining into the deepest points of her emotional reservoir. To trust her patience is to trust that when the Sun is warm enough, the ice will melt and she will move with great care—for the depth of her emotions will be carried to the edges of time and flow back to source. Trust in her patience that we are moving on time, for all is flowing back to the center of creation.

Poem #2

The blueprint for a new tree is imprinted in the leaves. Maybe this is the way with our bodies, each have a blueprint of the tree of life, or the kingdom of heaven. These leaves that fall never touch the ground, but glide and merge in a sphere. Where life and death merge represents a new world, one of eternal life, the everlasting kingdom. New roots are born from this world between dimensions, and here we have the image of the 5-D world perhaps born from the blueprint of the Tree of Life—from its leaves, new life.

From the new life come branches that inter- twine to create a new forest. A new forest meant to support new life for the 5-D planet. The tree of life is our body, and a new body is being born from the sphere. This may symbolize that the new bodies are becoming immortal, and we are forming roots in this new world. When we do so, our bodies will evolve, our shadows will be suffocated. Despair will be present, until we allow the healing energy to flow through us, and this is symbolized by the green man returning. Green man brings life everlasting.

April 15th, 2021

On a personal note, the tone was one of accep- tance. I can accept that I chose to be here, and what that means is to work through my hurt. The road is one of wanting, where people are driven by their wants and desires. Raindrops of violet fire symbol- ize a cleansing wash. To be wrapped in pink means to surround myself with unconditional Love—and this process is pivotal on the journey. Self-care and self-love are important when surrendering from the wants and desires. Wherever we are on our journey, to look at the hurts is one part. Another part is to own the hurts and find meaning. This process is to allow, accept, appreciate, which is the foundation of the walkway in the sky. The moon symbolizes reflection, and in reflecting, the dark roots within us can be found. We can surrender these roots to the Sun. Grief will come, and part of ourselves will be left behind, but finding meaning for the hurt will bring about new growth and expansion. The chaos can feel like uncertainty, part of our identity has been left behind. In its absence, who are we? What can we be but full of hope; and the bridge between worlds and words will be built. From the tears, light itself will grow.

April 22nd, 2021

Shadows of the mind hide in our crowns and prey on our connection to source. The paper tigers image is meant to show that the shadow shifts shapes to run from who it truly is, from our true essence. The prey is time, as if time itself will wear down the bodies. The shadow wants to climb the tallest tree, the biggest challenge. The shadow wants to conquer the great challenges, to move as if chased by time, from one challenge to the next. The shadow would want to conquer even the illusion of time. To climb that height, and only find that you have climbed sideways, is to be the shadows, up and down have lost meaning, feelings don't mean anything.

The shadows of the mind can travel everywhere in the world where the sun is dark. The shadow swoops down to the owl, a guide from the sky, who reveals that the shadow shifts shapes away from the truth of its essence. In the mind, the shadows travel to where we think we need to travel, and they pick the route we think we need to travel.

The shadows, in this thinking, can travel everywhere in the realm of the shadows. When we are present in our true essence, we can only be here, in the now moment. The shadowy sun does not show the truth, the truth that could strip away the false pieces of us constructed by our mind. Within our own forest floor, we can see that fire dances within us—our true essence that brings warmth to our being. The truth of our essence is that we have the smile of distant galaxies within us. The shadows of the mind have us believe otherwise. Through our hearts, we can connect with everything true within us. The poem represents a realization. The prey is the shadow of our minds. If we tap into that fire, we can disarm the shadows and see that we are home.

April 29th, 2021

A great amount of willpower is needed to maintain a certain appearance of royalty. The forgotten one, she sits on the throne, and she must maintain an angelic appearance. Her warrior is coming alive with her violet fire. When she remembers, and the memory returns to the world, the Divine feminine will burst forth with water to wash over the world.

The memory is that it is the seed that holds the cup, the egg that holds the ether, the feminine that holds the masculine, not the other way around, as the religions of man would like us to believe. This Divine Feminine will reverse the cycle, and from form we shall return to formless.

April 29th, 2021

For Brigette, this poem came through one night after work. Wild feathers plucked from the wing of the moon, which suggests she is flying a similar path as the moon. In her silence she is radiant. She is the owl, a messenger who travels between dimensions. She draws from the energy of the Sun and infuses it with her essence. The poem suggests a potential role for her, to help people understand and learn more about themselves.

May 10th, 2021

Poem #1

This poem was for Jaimee, channeled as guidance. The directions are veiled in mystery—we wondered if she was to travel to a location in the physical realm, or if it was work for the spiritual realm.

Aspects of the spiritual came through. The square with people who are driven by the need to succeed is evident from the eye of the tiger. People thirst for the kind of success that brings fortunes. The creative juices involved in our determination for life needs to be cleansed. Flush the gates, the line suggests to cleanse the source of that determination. To me, when dropped, the meaning is that interest is lost. Fortunes of man are left behind, as was the magic of old. The feeling is that a shift is coming, and the source of determination will be changing. What man considers fortunes will be changing, we will be moving away from using currency. Magic filled the people of old, their spirits lived the way of the drum, and this was their currency. If we have moved from the magic of old to the current currencies, where are we headed next? Energy is a currency. To compare to the magic of old, perhaps man moved from worshipping the moon to worshipping possessions. This then seems like guidance of what Jaimee can clear from the world. Her role as Mother Inanna involved birthing the new world, and in that role she was to make the choice of what ways of living would be supported, and what kind of ways should be deconstructed. A mother's role is in the magic of her womb. How to make that discernment? The truth is in the vibrations. What drives man to thirst for things may be due to the critters in what man consumes on a daily basis. When she fills the space with her Love, those critters will have nothing to feed on. The poem ends with a word of caution.

Those people who have been rid of critters will feed on bark, which does not seem to contain much substance. Perhaps symbolic that those people will feed on the thing that once caused the critter. Though they have been freed of the critter, the habit remains the same. They eat what easily falls to them from the sky. When they hunger for more, and begin reaching for the sky, which could be symbolic of them continuing to climb the sky with the same habits, she is to take a leap of faith and jump ship. Leave the ship behind, shake things up.

Poem #2

This poem highlights the test of time. A natural shift is meant when referring to Lakes created by time. The structures of man mean to prevent these natural shifts from occurring across the planet. It also refers to a global shift that is about to occur. The shift will be on the physical plane, across the planet, and also within. Craters of the moon is a symbol, we have within us all the elements of creation, our own living waters. The living water is a symbol of the Divine Feminine, as is the moon. The living water is a sacred place within our bodies, one represented by the womb, the place from which we create and nourish our creations. The living water also washes away from within us that which we no longer wish to create, or lend our nourishing energies to. It helps with releasing, and is associated with cleansing emotions stuck within the body. It is a natural regenerative process, and can wash away old hurts and wounds. In our current way of life, in society, man has built a way of life separated from emotion.

Test your waters, step beyond your comfort zone. Filter the experiences you have already had, within each of us is this abundant forest. Minerals from above, the message is about the nourishing realizations from your connection to source. Dew from the rocks, your connectedness with Earth, your nourishment from Mother. To unwind from the cloth is to be genuine and vulnerable. To be vulnerable is to let go of the pain, the hurts, and wounds.

You no longer need armor for your defenses. To be defensive is to enter with the intention you have something to prove. We journey to the heavens, where we no longer need to prove ourselves or compete to make an impact on the planet. On this journey, we are letting go and allowing all things related to the physical plane to be washed away. Our steps are becoming lighter, and so we will need less of the heavier densities. This is a blessing, one that we are all deserving of as children of God.

May 15th, 2021

Poem #1

This poem refers to a ceremony that Jaimee was to participate in. She was to go on a Hill

Quest. The Hill Quest is a Native American cere-
mony and is sacred. Jaimee was to let the tests fall
away, in preparation for ceremony, to overcome
the tests as she receives guidance for the next steps
of her journey. The hills will whisper to her, she
will commune with Spirit. She felt the rumbling
of the buffalo. In her belly, she felt the purging of
Earth as she too was being prepared to birth a new
world. She will dance a new path among the stars.
With a fiery passion, her heels will catch fire and
shake loose the tar from the shingles. This sym-
bolizes an awakening, shaking loose the hardened
ceilings or roofs of peoples' homes so they may see
the truth—that we are journeying to the sky. The
people in every home will see and have a chance to
remember where they came from. She will be the
catalyst for this awakening.

Poem #2

From where the ideas for the creation of each
animal had originated a new palette for creation is
being born. The codes and the DNA will be
blended, and from these unique animals, light will
be quantified and truly magnificent creations will
shine. All beings will be upgraded. She is decorated
in time, and space honors her, for she will create that
which matters. Space yields to her; she has freed
space and time.

The infinite is the new hourglass; the sand represents the creation of time. Everything is evolving with the new space, and all that matters will be supported. All that matters will be precious. The poem refers to a point in time when that which first created life will fold back into creation. Jaimee is being prepared for this new creation process. She will hear the vibrations and frequencies. She will have the ability to indent on the gel matrix and shape the new course of creation from that which approaches her to be included in the new creation. The space is infinite; there will be space for all who wish to join.

May 26th, 2021

Poem #1

The melody is a dance between masculine and feminine. Both bloom and complement one another. Pink and blue also seem to represent youth. The fountain of youth hears this growing process, and shadows long forgotten lift into the sky. Probably the youth refers to us who are spiritually young and have brushed shadows beneath the rug because we were unsure of what to do with them. The way the shadows are set free suggests a shape, a certain flow of the universe. From this flow, and returning of shadows to the sky, the dark roots disintegrate and crumble.

Their message is sent far and wide. Perhaps the shadows represent lifetimes of suppression and disempowerment. The simplicity of letting those shadows free signals to the universe a message of hope, that freedom and sovereignty are possible. The moon's light will bubble; and the message is that a fire is in the reflection of how we have been treated, how we interact with one another, how we connect to Earth. This fire is meant as a righteous anger, one to bring about change.

This likeness will be abundant in that many will feel that same call. This calling comes from her heart, her Love to see everyone evolve in freedom and sovereignty, free to be the best versions of their selves. This space will be the abundance of the new universe, molded from the curvature of her heart. Through Love, the flow of the old tunnel will be transmuted.

Poem #2

Where to look? Pests and critters have pulled her attention here and there. She sees with wisdom, and the hammer falls. She must see with a look that parts the distractions. Where is it going, in what direction is she meant to travel? She seeks these answers, because for so long she has been distracted with clearing out the underworld, weathering attacks from others, members of the community coming and going.

When she looks through it all, the guidance is to only glance. Otherwise the mind may become caught in all the details. That is truth for everyone. When gaining such clarity in our own lives, glance, for our vessels will store the locations, and by the grace and will of God we will find the way. Trust, it is a message of trust. If we allow our minds to take over, we may become lost in where we think we need to go—always doubting and second guessing. The stories of our roots will come to surface, and when we gain clarity of our direction, those stories remind us of where we've been, and the character we have developed that has helped us along the way. The wisdom has come from the trail of tears that was cut by our past hurts. On this trail are pieces of the truth of who we are and where we have always been headed.

Her wounds are great; they are the hurts of the Divine Feminine. The message is to plant yourself in the mud created by your tears, and find the meaning of the hurt. She is doing that, and from her wounds, she is moving the wind and creating a new standard of accountability. The standard is born from the center, the most sacred of all places, the heart. Where the direction is pointing may be many destinations. Lay quietly, and they will also meet your soul. Let the wind blow you to the road of life and travel by way of your heart. Scars may be re-opened, and the mend from standing back up will tear—there is no easy fix, this journey will be painful. What is Love without pain, but a library without books? The sun will ease the aches and refresh the smile. The sun will be re-energizing. The sun within will be re-energizing. To sun gaze can be very cleansing.

June 4th, 2021

The poem highlights the folly of titles. Perhaps the titles we place on people or objects act as masks for issues that need to be addressed within. When we place that title as a quick fix to mend the issue, the quick fix can lead one to believe that they can achieve great things overnight. But if the dream is big, goals must be set, and work must be put in. With vigor, the fire sees what needs to be completed and works quickly to blaze a path.

Green acres lends itself to an image of a natural way of living. Personally, it connected me with the memory of an old show that I once watched titled Green Acres. In the show, the man who spent his life in the big city is inspired to live a farm life. He is enthusiastic about calling himself a farmer, and is quick to buy much land and plant many things. But he encounters many troubles because of his lack of experience and wisdom with farming. What this poem suggests is that the old ways of being separated from the abundance and wisdom of connecting to Earth are to be composted. Through this awakening, no one will rain on the parade, so to speak. We are awakening to a creation larger than the world we create from our troubles. What is coming will pierce the reality that we have become accustomed to living in. There is nothing to fear, the OM represents the one true infinite creator, and those whose ears have been opened will hear and will be unafraid. Between the stars, hope fills the space. Fill yourself with light until nothing of the transition, of the awakening, burdens you, and you can hear this hope by simply being. The reminder is to also be still and allow your cup to overflow, take in the joy of life.

Poem #2

The beginning of this poem feels like a fairytale. Only this story is not meant to turn into a nightmare. The reminder is to check in with ourselves and ensure that we are prepared for the final dance. As we begin to check with ourselves, we should check our pockets, for our winning lottery tickets have been delivered. The numbers that matter have been in our hearts. This is to remind us to have faith in ourselves. We will have abundance beyond what we can comprehend with our eyes. Be ready for the ignition, the poem is reminding us. Fill yourselves with the light until the darkness is simply a hairstyle in which you can mold and shift in any way, which sounds like mastery and self-control.

July 2ⁿᵈ, 2021

Around this time, Jaimee was traveling to the Badlands. She was completing work on the grid and putting to rest a dark force that had prevented light from reaching sacred sites on the grid. While away on her travels, this message came through. It came through with a rhythm. The first verse highlights a victory of sorts. She is holding high her heart, as if to announce that light was returning to the grid. The second verse highlights the pearly gates opening. The feeling was that the advice would be for the next leg of her journey. The rabbit hole suggests connections with the popular children's story. She would have to journey down the rabbit hole, and encounter a white hat. The symbol refers to someone who is working behind the scenes, as an ally to the light. The feeling is a male might be working among the white hats. Perhaps it was a reminder to be mindful about whom she should trust when connecting with people working behind the scenes. To attach a kite to the sky feels like a representation of a leap of faith, in some way, that will get caught in the wind. The leap of faith would lead to the heavenly gates opening.

July 10th, 2021

The first few lines of this poem feel like lives of ancient civilizations, part of a burial ritual. In this context, the feeling is one of wiping the sword clean of whoever was handling it, and from whatever purpose. Now that the cleansing has occurred, those who went through the process are light enough to feel the veil as if it were the clouds above their heads. In the eleventh hour, we are close to midnight on the awakening countdown. With the veil above, pressure is felt—silent explosions, or fires, perhaps within, are occurring. Destruction of the old, and in the pines, which symbolize the divine masculine, bells signify new changes. The Christ consciousness, represented in the golden pinecone, would be born. The sun and the moon are united. This foretells of a period of great unity. The cube is symbolic of the energetic grid of Earth. The ethereal side, behind the veil, will be in alignment with where humanity will be. The fifth pillar is the fifth dimension, and will open from the heart of the planet. As to transform from the story of the Tree of Life, peace will come, wrapped as the gift from the past. As if to say the history of events regarding the tree of life was a gift from creator, meant for the purpose of learning. The future will reap the reward, as peace will be sewn together by many truths.

Her test is the one that will mean for all tests to come undone. She has made the sacrifice, the truest of all tests. The quest begins with her heart. She is the passion for the quest. The quest is to become Love, it is her destiny.

July 26ᵗʰ, 2021

In this poem, the journey is signified as running laps. The laps are infinite, because the journey towards the one true infinite creator is an infinite journey. Walking in place has the feel that the journey is spiritual in nature. The race of smoke and fumes is the rat race of survival that has become modern society. This awakening we are coming into is like holding a mirror to the kindling to see how we busy our hands for survival, and the spiritual journey will free us.

Bees and blue birds are symbols of nourishment and expression. The swallows represent to sing your song, or truth. It is through those who embrace the ways of these animals we can gather where the moonlight hides, and in private, speak our prayers. The message is that if we look to the way our guides, the bees, blue birds, and swallows, are behaving, they are showing us a way to live in harmony with Earth and nature. If we learn to live this way, perhaps we can share our burdens and hopes for the future in the privacy of prayer. In this way, we can surrender everything to God, and live in harmony with creation.

The next message is announcing that when the veil falls, our inner demons will be on the run. The meaning is that for all who are awake to the spiritual journey, their inner demons will be agitated. The beast represents Mother Nature. Her fiery dance will come in seasons, and the seasons will be parted by the clouds. This is meaning that the rhythms of life will be shaken, and this is meant to shake loose the old, and to allow the new.

We are on the verge of a massive awakening event, and the rocking chair is a metaphor to describe the readiness of the masses. The image is that the masses are near the edge of the chair and near a full tilt into a massive shift; suddenly they lean back and pull away from a massive event.

The message is that this motion can continue until the floorboards turn to dust, and either way, the kingdom of heaven will come to Earth. The poem is referring to Jaimee, she will be dancing on the sky. The truth is she has sacrificed her ascension to stay and help humanity move towards a collective ascension. The "either way" suggests that humanity could be leaning back on that rocking chair, and when kingdom comes, those who are unawake will have to continue their journey elsewhere. No matter the dance, creation will be all the brighter.

August 1ˢᵗ, 2021

The birthday poem describes a beautiful wedding. The vows suggest that the four, Mother and Father Creator, Mother Inanna and Father Yeshua, are becoming two. That means Mother Creator and Mother Inanna are becoming one, and this same merging is happening between Father Creator and Father Yeshua. Then the two are joining in unity to unite the masculine and feminine. All mothers will come undone, for there will be one mother through which the new world will be born. She will be carried in the wind, to create in a way that has never been done before. The ending is guidance for her, reminding her that where her heart shines, the path is true. The path is true because the path is her.

September 10ᵗʰ, 2021

Often I lay in bed when these sensations arrive. The event brought feelings of being home, and it brought sadness, but then hope that home will be coming to Earth. The series of prose that follows were inspired through my heart, channeled from Father Yeshua. Love tells many stories, and can show us, through our own stories, how wide the arms of Love can stretch.

October 1ˢᵗ, 2021

This poem speaks about the wave of ascension. With the tide, what has come to be is the ages that have gathered to be seen, and processed. Her belly rumbles as she goes through this process. Mother

Inanna is the whale, and Father Yeshua the dolphin. Their litter brings tears to his eyes, he is proud. Whenever I mean to connect with Father Yeshua, I feel his energy as a proud father. In this message, he is proud because their fins are strong. As they learn to swim; they are uncovering the old bits and pieces beneath the sands of time. The meaning is that they are focused on healing from the ancient lives. I have felt the call on a personal level. I have become more aware that I have been calling out to the universe, wanting to be whole again. The ancient wounds have been wiped clean, and the one true infinite creator has given us the opportunity to heal and learn from the past. How amazing to hear that the ancient stories, written in stone, have been cleared.

This gives hope to redemption, that the one true infinite creator will forgive all who seek to release their skeletons. In this poem, the skeletons are referred to in Jaimee's closet. Creation is sacred, and the old creations were held onto, but are now being cleared. Without the burden of these skeletons, she can relax. Her frequency is changing, and we will feel that in the way she approaches life. To let go of this world, she is traveling to a higher octave, to a place of Love unlike anything this world has ever seen, and she will be bringing that love back to this world. That will be the return of the sacred heart. The end is a message of passion, that no matter the days that are between her and Yeshua, they are but a breath away from being together in Love everlasting. Between the two, this life is transpiring, and so the journey is one of joy, and to make the journey is to walk with hope, hope for union of humanity, of masculine and feminine, hope for the remembrance of oneness.

October 6th, 2021

This poem was meant for guidance for me. The guidance is that when the realizations come, divine knowing will rain on my vision of reality. Aspects of my life that I have planted seeds for are floating in the wind, and the inspiration for the next move will come to me soft like a whisper, and the knowing is that I need only make soft, gentle movements to reach out and grasp the seeds. Trusting in that knowing will bring grace to my movements. In this soft gentleness, sweetness will be born from my heart. Allow myself to unfold is the message. Become the sweetness, and sense the colors of my soul. The bends represent the changes that come in life, and the guidance is to be gentle with myself through the changes, to allow myself time to curve, rather than a sudden bend. Magic is in my hands, and to tickle life seems to represent the way I can take life by the hand and arrange the things that come into my life. Even though I may not see the changes in how I am becoming a man, the message is to listen to my heart. Again, to know that to the core, I am the man that I am becoming. I am human, and on my journey, I am remembering that my humanity and my divinity go hand in hand, and like two worlds, are merging. With that merging comes the reminder to embrace the tears of my mistakes, and to know that new opportunities and new choices will come.

The image of a galaxy existing inside of my being shows how expansive I am—that we are vast inside of our human bodies. That too serves as a good reminder what a gift God has given us in these bodies. In fact, to add to the amazing element of that truth is that through eternity, a beginning and an ending exist within our bodies. If we look within, we may see that rooms exist. The message is to allow the flowers and blooms to fill these rooms and to soak in the scent of our own growth. To me, this message means to have pride and ownership in the new growth. Perhaps at this point in the journey, it may seem like attention is given to what is next to shed or leave behind, always to the next change, but we need balance. To find that balance is to also practice self-love and embrace what is already here, the person that I am.

November 11th, 2021

Prophecy

The prophecy is foretelling a major flip. The major change is that time will be no more. Through the transition, God will be reaching through the veil to protect all who are awake and ready to transition to the new world. Death and rebirth are parts of this process. The old world will melt away and be turned to dust, and carried through the eye of the universe. It is an event that will bring about cause for celebration, where dust will turn to gowns and stars. Father Yeshua and Mother Inanna will share the dance. She will have the first step, for wherever she steps, everyone will follow. Miracles will follow; creation will be born from her word, if she chooses. Wisdom will be returning when creation unreturns. The prophecy is mystical in nature and reminds me of the agnostic texts. Her word will be potent; it will breathe form to the formless. Unity is felt here, for the formless is the masculine, the consciousness. The universe is balancing its creation, what comes through the formless is now going through the form to return to the formless. The unity will bring knowledge of this creative process. Wisdom is what is meant to be unspoken, heard by those with ears to hear in the silence. Creation has lived and died, been destroyed and reborn, and all who have come since origin have within them pieces of the wisdom and knowledge of oneness. Where we fit together, we will unbecome as one, and we will be one.

Poem

We are at the dawn of a great awakening. Great ability for creation will be granted to those not using hammers to force situations/people into their reality. Any energetic blocks are meant for churning, to let things build, and during those moments, we do not need to work to the bone. The awakening will bring to light the greater power of the kingdom of Heaven. The wind, behind the scenes, is moving a great deal of pieces into place for the collective.

Rewards and blessings will not be left behind. They will be rewards born from the heavens. As we transition into the new world, this message is re-assurance that hope exists for the seeds we plant. As long as we are trusting for them to ripen in the soil, meaning to allow ourselves and our dreams to unfold with patience. The seeds will zoom away, and lift us away from the torrents of emotions that were the 3-D world. The only disaster is the fear that your beginnings will end before you have started. Humanity is on this teeter totter, swinging towards a collective awakening, but at times falling backwards.

The launch highlights the awakening, how close we have come as a collective. An unprecedented amount of angelic and star brothers and sisters are here around the planet to offer help in this process. When the Sun sets on this endeavor, we will meet on the fields of time, together between the end and the beginning. We are going to celebrate our freedom from time. Freedom will rain until the healing is complete. Green symbolizes healing. The ride will be like a roller coaster, the message is to

ride the tide—listen for the angels, and they will
bring messages for further guidance and hope.

November 22nd, 2021

Poem

This poem comes during a potent gateway
from 11/11 to 11/22. To stay locked away, to lock
your heart away, is to prevent that which is being
awakened. The heart consciousness is the purity
within us that is represented by the sheep. To have
no wool is to be vulnerable, and the transition will
be easier if vulnerable. The maiden is the symbol for
who will be guiding us through the awakening.

The rebirth comes, and with it the coming of
the Feminine consciousness, the Christ embod-
ied in the rose. The wind brings destruction and
change on a collective scale, and within. Her love
softens the blow, and to sense the age of the stem
is to widen awareness and see how magnificent
death can be. Whether it is a physical or spiritual
death, the rose shows us it is a tiny wrinkle on the
fold of life. Love is standing against time. What
does time know but to move forward and back-
ward, to measure the distance between the begin-
ning and the end? Love has seen it come and go,
and experiences the memory of each growth, its
ampleness, and it knows the curvature like a map.
Love understands the depth of its creation.

Where time measures the beginning and the ending of the rose, and measures its wrinkles, nothing matches the measure of the heart. The heart sees that although the leaves tilt, the beauty never wilts. The beauty is in the grace of returning from when it came, to celebrate its victory over time. Where the watch measures time as cold and calculated, the heart sees beauty, warmth, ampleness, and holds memories and understands the curves that represent the map of its growth. This is the heart consciousness put in an image opposite consciousness that is separated from the heart. As time unzips and life unfolds, the heart of creation will move to worlds far, far away, where time cannot measure it.

Prophecy

The second prophecy tells of another mystical experience. Where light moved from a gentle whisper, language was created. Again, this is an image from the formless to form. Symbols were born from language, and gave language meaning. A form was born from the formless and gave meaning to the formless. Language of the formless created knowledge, and all who had knowledge of their formless selves had the ability to receive the wisdom of their form. From knowledge itself, wisdom was born. Life was whispered into creation. From form came the purpose and meaning of having knowledge and wisdom. "They became life, and from Life came Love."

From the formless was born a vessel to transform life. Love, then, is like transforming the knowledge of living into wisdom. But that would not be possible without a vessel. When breath first came, the wisdom of its existence, it knew that it could breathe. At the exhale, the flame of its existence was extinguished, and this new knowledge brought surprises. From the wisdom that it could be created and extinguished, the void of the formless gave birth to the voidless form, and eyes were born. The edges remained unknown, and though it had eyes to see, it knew its limitlessness. Because it could not see through or know the limits of eternity, the wisdom of not knowing was born. This is the trend of life being transformed by the developing vessel of form. New life was born in that void of not knowing, which is the void of wisdom. The stories of old contain this content, the stories of how creation came to be. What stories will come from the new? We are nearing the final chapters.

The stories that remain untold are those that slipped beneath the void. Creation has reached a point of rebound, which feels like Life having experienced all that those in the void could not know. Imperfections from this not knowing are embraced by those with bodies. Humans embraced the flaws and imperfections, and it was humans who made aware to the void the knowledge and wisdom of the voidless. Through Love, we can accept the flaws of living and receive wisdom from our existence. From life in the voidless came pain, sadness, grief, anger, despair, worry, doubt, but also joy, happiness, bliss, peace, and Love.

When the shift occurs, top will become bottom, and the silence of the void will greet the whisper, the language that gave meaning to the voidless. To those in the void, we are thought of as the voidless. But it is because we exist at all that they have reason to think and know and communicate with us. New meaning will be given as the symbol is reborn. We are reaching a point where life has experienced the fullness of its voidless creation and is rebounding to the void. Through Love, all has been accepted, and all our wounds are being washed away. Through Love we are journeying to become one with creation through full acceptance of our perfectly imperfect selves—where and when the voidless and void will be one.

November 24th, 2021

The touching stone feels old and sacred, a site used for prayer. The feeling of this poem is one of traveling. References to games provide the atmosphere of celebration and nostalgia. Tents also suggest a temporary residence. This connects to the final move being in play, suggesting one final move before finding permanent grounds and moving on from the old games. This may be a reference to the 4-D holding ground that we have been in until we reach 5-D. As the final move is being prepared, the message is to reframe how you see things, and to reminisce over the sweet times.

Everything is ready, and the cakes are the rewards, meant to be sent through the cars, which symbolize ships. As mentioned in the past, rewards and manifested situations will be brought through to the new world. They will be sent with precision, to the stars, meaning you will have these rewards in the heavens. In the stars, our brothers and sisters await our return.

The seas will rise, and a great purging will take place. During this purge, the seasons will be changing. Though the changes are occurring, the message is urging to give thanks, and give prayers and wishes. Water can be utilized to amplify the prayers. What answers that arrive might surprise in the form of butterflies, which symbolize transformation.

To sit near candlelight, for the wicking hour, means to sit and collect thoughts and reflect on the day while winding down. We are at that point in the journey, and the time to transport to our next step is near. Rest well; the feeling is that rest will be needed for the final leg. Much work is to be done in the final leg.

December 2nd, 2021

What is mentioned in this poem is the ending of some dark practices on Earth. The beginning sounds like Father Yeshua and Mother Inanna, their emblem flashes in the stars as superheroes here to bring justice to the tots involved behind the scenes in show business. The child sex trade in show business will come to light, but until then, the message is that the curtains will be pulled shut and the practice will be ended.

The next part reads like directions for Jaimee. All those with eyes to hear, meaning to sense beyond the veil, will sense what Jaimee has completed earlier in the year when she traveled out west. She reclaimed the grid near the stone heads, and eliminated the dark beings and breathed light into it.

At this point in time, she is to follow that rabbit hole, remotely, and travel to the core. By expanding the opening and stretching the funnel, she is helping Mother Gaia to release the worries of the world. Since she is merged with Mother Gaia, she is also releasing and feeling these purges.

She is the living vessel who is assisting with the worries of the world. She will share stories of the work done beyond the veil. How fragile and thin the veil is becoming, and as it thins, she is closer to her unity with her beloved Yeshua. Wedding bells chime, and she is the trumpeter's swan.

As a tributary to meet the band, she is to undergo a death of sorts, or perhaps to honor the flow to begin to roll with anything that could happen. The fairytale ending is drawing near. The lead guitarist will play under her reflection. When the clock strikes midnight, and the game is near the ending, there will be a window of time before the veil thickens and all returns to stone.

The poem pivots to the game metaphor, and there is meaning in how the shot is taken and the nature of the shot. The shots less taken give meaning and value to the shots that are taken. The winning shot seems like the shot at a collective ascension, a shot to bring forward all of humanity at once. The shot will be taken from the backboard rather than a direct approach. The backboard is to provide a buffer and to increase the chances of a collective ascension. In the fairytale ending, the rain will come, for a final cleanse. Behind the veil, and behind the sun, the bridge to eternity will be opened.

December 10th, 2021

Merriment fills this poem. As the holidays draw closer, this message brings glad tidings. The words paint the scene of a joyous occasion, and many sweet treats are on the way. These treats feel like rewards. For those who succeeded under the eye of appraisal, and whose cups are running empty, gifts will be delivered, and they are sure to make you cry. Meanwhile, our star brothers and sisters are watching. While the world is dazed in wonder, they will be shaken and a final cleansing will take place. All that remains from the past will be shaken loose—cleared for the new upgrades and expansion.

December 21st, 2021

Poem #1

The opening of this poem feels like a declaration of freedom. The call that comes to us all is meant to stir something within us and awaken our passion to follow our destiny. These winds of change will be the winds that guide people to the destiny they agreed to upon coming to Earth. The course is being plotted, Jaimee (Mother Inanna), is the eagle here. The condor is Father Yeshua. A prophecy of the eagle and condor exists. In the prophecy, the condor will latch onto the eagle and bring it to new heights. In this poem, the eagle is plotting the course, seeing but faint outlines. Father Yeshua is circling from the heavens, making light his presence of knowing what is to come. The message for Jaimee is to trust her heart and choose what speaks to her. For many of us, this is a potent message. Life has a way of moving, sometimes sunny days come, other days are cloudy. When the clouds of doubt are thick like fog, and navigating our way through life becomes challenging, to remember the kids is to remember our own purity and innocence within. Our inner child knows the way and has the sunshine of the creator.

In that freedom, we will know what it feels like to see the chief of the Sun waiting for the inspiration that moves our lives to deliver warmth throughout our entire beings. How will we know which way to travel? To follow our emotions is symbolized with the water and the earth. The deepest trenches, from our deepest emotions comes that new fifth element, Love.

Symbolized here as Jaimee, and Mother Inanna, Love will nourish all that we are in our beings. As we ascend, our beings are being reborn in the sky. The breaking of formation is symbolic of following our inner guidance, our inner truths. When we begin to do that, the Sun will be buried into the fabric of our identity. Perhaps we follow others because we have not searched for our own truth, and for the process to begin, that which needs to come undone must be done within.

The poem describes a journey taken by Mother Inanna and Father Yeshua, which at this point have merged with Mother Creator and Father Creator, and their actions create ripple effects that set the standard by which creation will follow. The standard is Love, and as we feel inward, we feel the journey already taken by our Divine Parents, and we too can begin to journey alongside them when we go within.

Prophecy

From this prophecy, the message is that no more stories will be told by time. The prophecy tells the oldest story of the creation of the universe. Parts of the void were unexplored. From the second prophecy, the void gave birth to the voidless. This prophecy fills gaps in that story. Here, we see the formation of gravity and time. The movement in the spaces between spaces was meaning that was spoken by no one, yet it was a vital life force energy, it was potential. An alchemical chamber formed, and from the second prophecy this was evidence from the transformational ability of life.

Life existed, so the formless gained form, and when light expanded, the infinite was born. Time was born, and it gave meaning to the infinite. The magnetic presence gave form to the formless in the form of shapes and faces. Gravity was born, and it gave meaning to the presence of form and the infinite. Balance existed between the void and voidless, like the flow and rhythm of a heartbeat. The heartbeat was the center of creation and the life force that breathed expansion into it.

From the sound of it, creation has headed toward the void and been re-created in the past. Perhaps it will always return to the void to be re-created. The message is suggesting that in this new upcoming experience of oneness with the creator, each of us will be equal creators. This next breath from the void will be a connection between that which is animated to move and the unmoving—all of creation will draw the light and transform its existence into wisdom. The heartbeat of creation will beat a final time and will collapse to nothing, and the unity of the two, void and voidless, masculine and feminine, will expand even wider and the transformational golden frequency energy will be at everyone's feet. We will all draw from the new core of the merging duality. The creator will be born through the body, and those with bodies will embody the creator in the fullness of void and voidless. We will be complete. No more stories will need to be told, we will create anew. With that new creation comes the responsibility of our creation, the accountability. The art shows the rabbit hole, and down the hole we go, making a conscious choice and knowing the weight of that choice.

December 24th, 2021

The beginning of the poem is setting the stage. The action is about to go live. With the heightened action, discernment is important. Leaders with no weights are like casting a hook and it floating near the surface. With no weight, it cannot reach the depths. Be discerning of what is on the surface, it may be all show and no meat, so to speak. Seek what is meant to be found, the truth is within you. Look to the heavens for help, they will answer when given the call. As the gifts come, know that with great reward comes great responsibility.

The rewards will bring new roles, and with those roles, new responsibilities. The next few lines refer to a potential timeline where Jaimee is brought home to Spirit, so she can help organize pieces from that side of the veil. No blame would be placed anywhere, it would not have been a gamble. The associates are the aces and will fill in any gaps at the ministry.

The divine feminine is on the rise, and she is the heir to the kingdom of heaven. Her water is her emotions and she speaks in light, of another language of love. When she speaks, her words give form to the light in her emotions—she speaks of the new world. Her words carry the high frequencies to anchor the new world. The source of those new frequencies will spread around the globe, and the four directions in the Spirit realm. Many will come, and those who are loyal to her Love will watch over the flow of things. Beings from the spirit side will want to influence matters, but those with discernment will protect the frequencies by knowing what to filter.

The last few lines suggest being mindful of how to walk during these times. To whisper with the wind is to not resist what destinies are coming to you. Walk with mindfulness, where you step will have great importance. Light meant for you will shine on certain steps, these are the steps meant for you, for your soul. Again, discernment will be an important skill. To ask, what am I feeling? Where is it coming from? Is it mine? These questions will help in the process of feeling what is yours and what is not.

January 8th, 2022

This poem touches on the merging of Mother Gaia and Mother Inanna. Jaimee is here as the embodiment of the two merging, and around these times she feels the quakes in her body. She feels the purging of those on the planet and the planet herself. Everything funnels through her and returns to source. The message is that Jaimee's diamond core is radiating light. The oceans are the emotions of the world being filtered through the fabric of her heart. The softness of her heart is helping to open portals. The water and fire from portals, and the elements, are jolting together. From the earth, we will feel the quakes—but it needs to happen—to charge her for the upcoming shifts. She and Mother Gaia will be shifting through portals in February. Filters will help to purify further. Our brothers and sisters from the stars are helping. Whatever darkness is left will be cleaned away. Everything will be cleared out. A light-hearted message is included in the checking of socks for anything left behind.

Not even a shred of doubt of turning back. We will be moving full speed ahead when light fills the gaps. Miracles are following Jaimee, and they will soon take flight. Three stars will shoot by on three different occasions. Three will be the green light. On Capitol Hill a new light will shine. The storm is coming, that is a reference to political events that will be taking place. The message is foretelling a leader, as the snow echoes in the approaching storm; the light will read a capital "T."

Messages in this manuscript tell of public events, events behind the veil—in spirit—and the spiritual journey within. This message refers to an event both behind the veil and in the public eye.

About the Author

James Vissers was born in Minnesota and raised on a dairy farm in Wisconsin. After the sudden passing of his father, due to a heart attack, the family farm was sold. After graduating high school, he went on to attend college in hopes of becoming a personal trainer. He aspired to help people improve their general health and wellness. Through the years of the grieving process, he rediscovered his creative side. He switched tracks in school to complete a degree in creative writing, and was inspired to work towards, and graduated with, a Masters of Art in Science Writing.

He felt a calling to express Divine truth to humanity. While working on his Masters, he lived at his childhood home and served as a caretaker for his mother and younger sister. His mother had been diagnosed with liver cancer. She is now in remission, and her health and wellness has returned. His sister has Down Syndrome, and from growing up with her, he became sensitive and attuned to connecting with a different kind of language. The language was energetic and universal.

As a young boy, he often connected with a Sasquatch guide who helped him through challenging moments. Following graduation from his Masters program, he answered a call and moved to

North Dakota, where he became a student and associate of Divine Healing Heart Ministry. He was following a path of healing, and expanding his growth and awareness. He is also a student learning about Native American ceremonies.

Currently, he is channeling and documenting messages from the Divine to assist in our collective awakening and ascension. He is passionate about developing and supporting humanitarian plans that help humanity evolve in a way that is for the highest good of all. He loves to read, write, meditate, and share laughs with family and friends. He is here to deliver this book: Transcending Form: Ascend to the Stars.

About the Illustrator

Rylee Slivicki, owner of Creative Rose, and Minister of Divine Healing Heart Ministry is a self taught spiritual artist that uses everything and anything (chalk, colored pencil, charcoal, paint, sculpture, wire, mix media, etc.) to bring love and light to this world.

She went to primary school at Dilworth-Glyndon-Felton, Minnesota where she was active in her school and community with dance, Girl Scouts, theater, track, speech, and art club. Rylee was always gifted growing up. When she was 14 her family moved to Wahpeton, ND to be more involved with Divine Healing Heart Ministry. It was at Divine Healing Heart Ministry where Rylee was taught and mentored to be a Reiki Healer by bringing balance to the mind body and spirit. Later she became a Reiki master, got her GED when she was 16, and started her own art business. Since then she has been recognized and taught by Native American Chiefs. She has also become a dedicated humanitarian along with her associates at Divine Healing Heart Ministry where she found a community of like-minded individuals who want to make a positive impact on this world.

Looking forward she is excited to become a more active spiritual mentor, and take her art to the streets with murals and chalk. She has always loved art because it gives individuals the ability to self express beyond words, and hopes to bring about change through art that speaks to the soul.

(Prophecy #3, The Universal Star of Mother Inanna, 12/25/21)

·

www.ingramcontent.com/pod-product-compliance
Lightning Source LLC
Chambersburg PA
CBHW041822090426
42811CB00010B/1076